Journal of International Doctoral Research (JIDR)

Journal of International Doctoral Research

CONTENTS

Volume 6, Number 1, 2017

JOURNAL OF INTERNATIONAL DOCTORAL RESEARCH

Sponsored by the International Doctoral Research Centre (www.idrcentre.org)

Volume 6, Number 1

Introduction and Welcome

The International Doctoral Research Centre (IDRC; www.idrcentre.org) was created by like-minded researchers who wish to promote excellence in doctoral and post-doctoral research. The IDRC publishes an annual journal: the Journal of International Doctoral Research (JIDR). The IDRC provides doctoral associates and experienced post-doctoral researchers with a forum for presenting and discussing their research. Specifically, the IDRC provides a forum for peer review of a researcher's current ideas and thoughts which enable him/her to formulate future research plans or unblock problems with current research. A benefit of the IDRC includes building a close network of experienced researchers. To submit a manuscript for blind peer review for publication to the JIDR, please forward to: jidr.submissions@idrcentre.org

This issue

This year we celebrate our journal's 6th anniversary. In 2014, after just two years of operations, we were honored with an important accreditation for all the hard work done by the Journal's authors, editorial review board members, and editors: the JIDR was given official accreditation status in Europe, specifically in the Norwegian academic publishing system. Our goal since then has been to maintain and develop such academic ranking status. Furthermore, we aim to continue to seek external recognitions for the JIDR and to continue to develop the impact of our publication within the international research community.

This 6th volume of the JIDR is devoted to a wide range of research themes, which are all linked to the concepts of management both implicitly and explicitly. Management research is no longer defined or confined to work and organizational studies. Today, management is at the interface of ways of thinking and acting in all aspects of our lives. The very history of management scholarship is rooted in the world of work and also with concern for employees well-being, as workers are not simply units of capital production, but also human beings. In this issue we use a management lens to look at some fundamental questions societies face today, such as ethics, successful counselling for well-being at work, the age of digitalization in the banking industry, public policies – what matters, health and well-being and recovering from life threatening illness and lastly, gender imbalance in paid work globally. The discussions in these articles highlight several recurring and yet under-researched issues in these fields. In the coming year, it is our vision to have the JIDR continue to publish a combination of manuscripts related to the theme of diversity in international research – We very much appreciate your support as we strive to develop the JIDR as an authoritative journal which publishes re- search both on empirical data collected for doctoral studies and post-doctoral research in an international context. The success and sustainability of our Journal depends on the number of quality manuscripts submitted for peer review. Our acceptance rate is between 25 % and 50 % each year. Consequently, we encourage you to invite colleagues to consider the JIDR as an excellent publication channel for academics.

All submissions by prospective authors will be handled efficiently by our blind peer review process, and will also be offered a similarity screening check. One of the great benefits to all authors who submit manuscripts to the JIDR is that no matter whether their work is accepted for publication or not, detailed one-to-one feedback on both content and language is always given. These are high quality helpful reviews that are designed to help authors improve their research methodology and manuscripts further.

As in prior years, we would like to take this opportunity to thank the JIDR advisory board members, reviewers and authors, who support the journal and help make it so successful. On a final note we greatly appreciate your support and as our readers. We hope this year's articles offer you new reflections upon the multifaceted concepts of 'diversity' and 'inclusion' within all we do in work and life.

My best regards on behalf of the editorial team

Dr ABM Abdullah

Editor

Manuscript Preparation

To help us with the submission process, please follow the preparation checklist prior to submitting your manuscript. Submissions may have to be returned to authors that do not adhere to the following guidelines. We thank you for your assistance.

Checklist

- Manuscripts should not have been previously published nor submitted to another journal for consideration. If the manuscript has appeared elsewhere, please ensure that you have permission for it to be published in the JIDR and that you acknowledge such a release (see the style guide).
- Please ensure that the electronic file is in Microsoft Word or RTF format.
- Please check that the text adheres to the stylistic and bibliographic requirements outlined below.
- Copyright notice: Please note: authors who submit a manuscript to the JIDR agree to grant the journal right of first publication. If your manuscript is published in the JIDR, you will still retain copyright ownership of your material but should generally acknowledge that the manuscript appeared in the JIDR with a proper citation.

Manuscript stylistic and bibliographic requirements

- As a guide, articles should be between 15 and 20 pages in total, including figures, graphs, charts, tables, references, etc.
- A title of not more than eight words should be provided.
- A brief autobiographical note should be supplied including full name, affiliation, e-mail address.
- Copyright release/acknowledgement (if necessary).
- Authors must supply an abstract of no more than 500 words.
- Although optional, authors are encouraged to provide up to six keywords which encapsulate the principal topics of the paper.
- Headings must be short, with a clear indication of the distinction between the hierarchy of headings. All headings are to be left justified. The first hierarchy is to be bolded, the second order of hierarchy is to be bolded and italicized, the third order is to be italicized but not bolded.
- Notes or footnotes should be used only if necessary and must be identified in the text by consecutive numbers, enclosed in square brackets and listed at the end of the article.
- All Figures (charts, diagrams, line drawings, web pages/screenshots) are to be embedded directly into the document.
- References to other publications must be in APA style and carefully checked for completeness, accuracy and consistency.

Silence Is Golden? The Case of two Whistleblowers in a Norwegian Municipality

Petter Gottschalk

BI Norwegian Business School, Oslo, Norway

ABSTRACT

Characteristics and experiences of whistleblowers are an important field of research for work and organizational psychology. Detection and prevention of misconduct and crime is dependent on people internally who are not afraid to speak up and tell about their observations. Two key employees in the municipality of Grimstad in Norway reported separately about critical financial incidents in procurement of health services. They were ignored by the perceived power elite in the municipality. At the time of writing this research article, both whistleblowers are on sick leave. This article presents two whistleblowers who – despite perceived retaliation and reprisals - are willing to do it again. They simply define it as part of their job.

Key Words: Deviant behavior, organizational opportunity, white-collar crime, convenience theory, whistleblowing, retaliation.

1. Introduction

Two key employees in the municipality of Grimstad in Norway reported separately about critical financial incidents in procurement of health services. They were ignored by the perceived power elite in the municipality. At the time of writing this research article, both whistleblowers are on sick leave (Berg, 2017).

Fortunately, there was a courageous control committee in the municipality that, after some ambiguity, addressed the case and continues to investigate procurement of health services.

An internal investigation by global accounting firm BDO (2016) of health services in Grimstad municipality had already been conducted. The 64-page review report for the control committee is dated December 7, 2016. The examiner did not get to the bottom of the case, partly because "almost all documentation relating to the procurement" is missing, and because there are "unusually many" of the persons that the examiner interviewed "who cannot remember important events" (quotes from the investigation report).

For half a year, further investigation was hampered by the perceived power elite in the municipality in an attempt to bring the matter to silence. Due to the thorough work of the control committee and considerable local media attention (e.g., Berg, 2016, 2017; Karlsen, 2017), it was decided at the municipal council meeting that the control committee should be provided sufficient funding to continue its internal investigation by hiring an external examiner. The examiner should focus on the contents of employees' e-mails concerning health service purchases, to which the BDO (2016) examiner had no access.

The case of two whistleblowers in the Norwegian municipality is interesting in light of research by Bjørkelo et al. (2011), who studied characteristics and experiences of self-reported whistleblowers in Norway. They found that whistleblowers reported low levels of retaliation at the same time as they reported less job satisfaction and more bullying at work than their non-reporting colleagues (Eriksen, 2017).

This article addresses the following research question: *What whistleblowing experiences can be derived from the case of two whistleblowers in a Norwegian municipality?* Empirical evidence was collected through interviews with whistleblowers, media reports, and municipality documents.

This research is important since "public procurement is extremely vulnerable to instances of fraud, corruption or waste due to the amount of money circulating between the public and the private sector" (Nesti, 2014: 62).

The article starts by defining internal investigations, as fraud examiners were hired by the municipality to investigate allegations by the whistleblowers. Next, a short description is presented of white-collar crime, which is at the core of whistleblowing allegations. Then, we return to the whistleblowing case in Grimstad municipality and present whistleblowing theories in the literature review. Finally, the Grimstad case is discussed based on the literature reviewed.

2. Internal Investigations

An internal investigation is about reconstructing events and sequence of events. The investigator is to find out what happened or did not happen, how it happened or did not happen, and who did what to make it happen or not happen (Brooks and Button, 2011; Button and Gee, 2013; Button et al., 2007; Schneider, 2006; Williams, 2005). An internal investigation is conducted by fraud examiners from law firms and auditing firms, and it is similar to a police investigation.

An investigation starts with a choice of knowledge strategy (categories of required expertise), information strategy (preferred information sources), method strategy (open or closed communication), configuration strategy (sequential or iterative procedure), and system strategy (digital search and selection). Knowledge strategy is about who will conduct the investigation. In the case of Grimstad were the main focus is on e-mails, the examiner must be an expert in digital search, content analysis, interviewing techniques and white-collar crime, rather than the law or municipal administration (Gottschalk, 2016).

The investigator's task is to describe actual circumstances within a particular topic or mandate. The investigation is intended to determine what actually happened in a particular case. An investigation is about revealing relevant facts. The objective is to provide actual and relevant information and describe them in such a way that responsible persons can make the best decisions on the consequences that the matter will have. The investigator must work at least as vigorously to prove innocence and lack of guilt as evidence of guilt. There should be no blame game unless it is rightfully detected (Lee and Robinson, 2000).

At the time of writing this article, the control committee in Grimstad municipality was to hire an external examiner to investigate e-mails concerning procurement of health services. However, e-mail is only one of many sources of information in an internal investigation. Other information sources include tips, interviews, and documents. The examiner must analyze e-mails by linking other sources of information to interpret text in emails. Many people in the municipality seemed to have useful information for the following investigation. Therefore, the perceived power elite in the municipality should facilitate the examiner's information collection and analysis.

The perceived power elite in the municipality believed that the most important thing was to get the case closed. However, a skilled investigator might reveal fraud, corruption or other forms of financial crime, which the local government would have to address after investigation completion and do something about. Therefore, a discussion occurred whether the councilor should be granted temporary leave of absence until the investigation was completed. It was also discussed whether the mayor should temporarily leave the helm to the deputy mayor (Berg, 2017).

3. White-Collar Crime

Economic crime committed by the elite in society through abuse of trust-based positions of power is called white-collar crime (Gottschalk, 2017; Sutherland, 1939, 1949, 1983). By misuse of their trusted positions in business, government and politics, white-collar criminals enrich themselves or the business to which they are affiliated. In an organizational context, white-collar criminals have the opportunity to commit financial crime and to conceal crime. White-collar criminals carry out embezzlement, tax evasion, corruption and other forms of economic crime.

White-collar crime is a unique area of criminology due to its atypical association with societal influence compared to other types of criminal offenses. White-collar crime is defined in its relationship to status, opportunity, and access. This is the offender-based perspective. In contrast, offense-based approaches to white-collar crime emphasize the actions and nature of the illegal act as the defining agent. In their comparison of the two approaches, Benson and Simpson (2015) discuss how offender-based definitions emphasize societal characteristics such as high social status, power, and respectability of the actor. Because status is not included in the definition of offense-based approaches and status is free to vary independently from the definition in most legislation, an offense-based approach allows measures of status to become external explanatory variables.

Benson and Simpson (2015) approach white-collar crime utilizing the opportunity perspective. They stress the idea that individuals with more opportunities to offend, with access to resources to offend, and that hold organizational positions of power are more likely to commit white-collar crime. Opportunities for crime are shaped and distributed according to the nature of economic and productive activities of various business and government sectors within society.

Benson and Simpson (2015) do not limit their opportunity perspective to activities in organizations. But they emphasize that opportunities are normally greater in an organizational context. Convenience theory, however, assumes that crime is committed in an organizational context to be labelled white-collar crime (Gottschalk, 2017). This is in line with Sutherland's (1939) original work, where he emphasized profession and position as key characteristics of offenders.

Gottschalk (2017) introduced convenience theory as an integrated explanation of white-collar crime, based on a number of theories from criminology and organizational behavior. Convenience is a concept that was theoretically mainly associated with efficiency in timesaving. Today, convenience is associated with a number of other characteristics, such as reduced effort and reduced pain. Convenience is associated with terms such as fast, easy, and safe. Convenience says something about attractiveness and accessibility (Sundström and Radon, 2015).

Public procurement corruption is one form of white-collar crime that involves a breach of trust or an abuse of position by federal, state or local government officials (Nestli, 2014). Elite public criminals can use the power and apparent legitimacy of their office to extort bribes or direct procurement to entities they control or from which they benefit. They can shape the environment by organizing procurement processes and formulating regulatory requirements. Private elites can indirectly achieve the same profitable results by suborning public officials to modify the environment to benefit the private party, for example by going to a non-bid, sole-source market (Gottschalk and Smith, 2016).

4. Case Study

This article presents a case study of whistleblowing intentions and experiences in a Norwegian municipality. Sources of information include fraud investigation reports (e.g., BDO, 2016), media coverage (e.g., Berg, 2016, 2017; Karlsen, 2017) as well as interviews with both whistleblowers. Elements from the literature review on whistleblowing (e.g., Bjørkelo, 2011; Eriksen, 2017; Mpho, 2017) are compared to case information.

Content analysis (Patrucco et al., 2017) is the research methodology applied in this study of various documents concerned with suspicion of white-collar crime in public procurement (Nestli, 2014). Content analysis is a procedure that identifies specific characteristics within texts attempting to make valid inferences (McClelland et al., 2010: 1259):

Content analysis assumes that language reflects how people understand their surroundings and reflects their cognitive processes.

This case study research is exploratory in its perspectives as it wonders whether or not silence is golden, or whistleblowing is the preferred option when wrongdoing and misconduct is observed.

The case study design in this research has the individual whistleblower as the unit of analysis. The case study as a research strategy is used to contribute to our knowledge of individual whistleblowing and to the whistleblowing literature. As indicated by Yin (2003: 2), the case study has long been a common research strategy in psychology and organizational behavior, and "the distinctive need for case studies arises out of the desire to understand complex social phenomena". Creswell (2003: 15) stresses that the researcher in case studies "explores in depth" one or more individuals.

5. Grimstad Case

In addition to suspected white-collar crime in the procurement of health care services, the municipal management in Grimstad also had to handle the whistleblowers. One of the notifiers engaged the country's leading whistleblowing expert as his attorney. In a sixteen-page letter, the lawyer takes a settlement of how the notifier had been treated. The lawyer makes a concrete claim for three hundred thousand Norwegian kroner (US 50.000 dollars) and announces that compensation may also be claimed (Berg, 2017).

A notifier or whistleblower is a person who believes to have discovered or uncovered and therefore notifies of critical circumstances or illegal activities in an organization in which he or she is employed or otherwise involved. A whistleblower was originally a person who witnessed a robbery and called attention by blowing a whistle. Today, the term is used of a person who calls attention to unacceptable conditions related to his or her own organization.

The other notifier hired an attorney who pointed out all the mistakes that the law firm working for the municipality should have made (Kluge, 2017). The law firm seems to have ended up with conclusions that the client preferred, such as denying access to e-mails and criticizing the whistleblower. Currently, the other notifier has not sued his employer.

The perceived power elite in Grimstad was suspected of systematic expulsion and retaliation (Berg, 2017; Eriksen, 2017), which is punishable in the criminal justice system in Norway. Local police and the central economic crime unit were considering a police investigation into both the health services procurement case as possible corruption and the expulsion and retaliation accusations.

There was suspicion of corruption, and the whistleblowers in favor of more investigation were hoping for answers. It would not come as a surprise to Grimstad inhabitants if corruption was detected. In a representative survey by the local newspaper, 3 out of 4 inhabitants suspected corruption in the municipality (Strand, 2017). As suggested by Nesti (2014), public procurement is extremely vulnerable to instances of fraud, corruption or waste due to the amount of money circulating between the public and the private sector.

A whistleblower is a person-based information source that can refer investigators to location-based, archive-based, and technology-based information sources in a case. A notifier is a person who notices something blameworthy, and who tells it to someone who can do something about the critical issue. A person is not a whistleblower if negatively affected by the critical issue as a victim.

In Norway, the government extended the protection of whistleblowers on July 1, 2017. Now temporary employees can also report about critical conditions. All businesses with five employees or more are obliged to prepare procedures for whistleblowing and protection of whistleblowers. Retaliation prevention as well as position security are further strengthened.

Whistleblowers are protected in Norway from reprisals in the Working Environment Act from 2005: "Employees have the right to notify about critical circumstances in the employer's business"; "Retaliation against an employee is prohibited"; and "If an employee discloses information that gives reason to believe that retribution has occurred; then it shall be assumed that such retaliation has actually taken place".

The notifier who later sued the municipality for retaliation in the summer of 2017 (Eriksen, 2017), started by sending a message of 1874 words to all members of the municipality board in Grimstad on February 12, 2017, where he blew the whistle. Among others, he wrote:

Of course, at this time, I have thought a lot about how it was possible for this organization to commit so extensive breach of legislation, own procurement rules, and ethical guidelines as this case has revealed. How was this possible on the basis of the audit's documentation in 2009 of major breaches of procurement legislation, the great erosion of this in 2010-2012, and the marketing of Grimstad municipality as a pioneer municipality in procurement? Why has nobody apparently put down the foot? Why did nobody blow the whistle before? There has been no lack of courses and knowledge about public procurement among executives in Grimstad municipality. And why has this happened so secretly? In a municipality that has not been reluctant to market itself with transparency? And what does it mean when so many executives apparently thought it appropriate to keep this case hidden from politicians elected and the public? That in an acute situation concerning placement of a user an action not according to the book can occur (in 2012) is understandable, but not that in 2017 similar services are purchased in complete conflict with laws and regulations.

Later in this article, the notifier who sued his employer is labeled B, while the other notifier is labeled A.

6. Literature Review

Whistleblowing involves revealing or exposing perceived negative secrets that an organization is involved in. Whistleblowing is an action by employees who believe that their business or colleague(s) are involved in activities of misconduct and financial crime, cause unnecessary harm, violate human rights or contribute to otherwise immoral offenses. Whistleblowing includes informing superiors, professional organizations, the public or some government agency of these activities (Mpho, 2017).

Ethical theories are concerned with egoism, deontology, and utilitarianism. According to Mpho (2017), the traditional ethical theory is that individuals aim to pursue their own self welfare. Individuals always act in their own self-interest. This theory might be rejected at whistleblowing because self-interest promotes selfishness. Many individuals think that being selfish is wrong, especially if it means that you are not considerate of others' wants and needs. Since egoism is based on the fundamentals of self-interest, and since there usually are no benefits to whistleblowing in most cases, there is no motive to reveal unethical or illegal acts by others. Only when there is something in it for the egoist, then whistleblowing can be an attractive action.

Deontology is an approach to ethics that focuses on the rightness or wrongness of actions themselves, as opposed to the rightness or wrongness of the consequences of those actions. Whistleblowing is carried out if it is considered the right thing to do.

Utilitarianism is only concerned with the outcome, while deontology is based on universalizing ones actions. In utilitarianism, the theme is to do an action which will benefit the greatest good for the greatest number of people. Whistleblowing may be supported by utilitarianism if it will benefit a significant number of people (Mpho, 2017).

Pittroff (2014: 124) applied legitimacy theory to explain the motivation to implement whistleblowing systems:

"By understanding whistle-blowing systems as an instrument that is desired by society, the legitimacy theory could be transferred to the whistle-blowing concept".

Central to legitimacy theory is a social contract, which implies that the existence of an organization depends on the boundaries and norms of the society. The social contract contains specific expectations of the society about the optimal behavior of an organization.

Rothwell and Baldwin (2007) applied ethical climate theory to study police whistleblowing versus the code of silence. Ethical climate is what organizational members perceive to be the ethical norms and identity of the organization. Study findings suggest that developing a friendly, team-interest ethical climate might enhance willingness to blow the whistle.

The case of two whistleblowers in the Norwegian municipality Grimstad is interesting in light of research by Bjørkelo et al. (2011), who studied characteristics and experiences of self-reported whistleblowers in Norway. They found that whistleblowers reported low levels of retaliation at the same time as they reported less job satisfaction and more bullying at work than their non-reporting colleagues. They asked the rhetorical question "Silence is golden?" that is repeated here, without any clear answer.

Uhl-Bien and Carsten (2007: 188) explain silence by obedience:

"All too often, hierarchical role expectations cause employees to assume they should not speak up for fear of being blamed and attacked for problems or issues they raise (e.g., "kill the messenger")".

Bjørkelo et al. (2011) studied whistleblower characteristics in terms of tenure, job level, job satisfaction, gender and age. Experiences related to whistleblowing were measured with nine questions, such as nature of whistleblowing, how long it was since they had blown the whistle, types of wrongdoing, who the wrongdoers were, whistleblowing channels, blown the whistle alone or in collaboration with others, effects on the reported wrongdoing, reactions to the wrongdoers, and what happened to them personally after they had blown the whistle.

Average tenure was 11 years, average age was 44 years, and job satisfaction was 4.1 on a multiple item scale from 1 (satisfied) to 7 (dissatisfied). Whistleblowers were more often a man

(52%), a leader (25%) or a union or personnel safety representative (24%), compared to non-whistleblowers.

Whistleblowers mainly used internal channels, either by only reporting internally or by first blowing the whistle inside the organization and later reporting to recipients outside the organization. Very few whistleblowers reported only to external sources or to someone outside the organization before they reported internally. The overall majority of whistleblowers had blown the whistle in their current job, and these were the only whistleblowers included in further analysis by Bjørkelo et al. (2011). Harassment was the most frequently reported type of wrongdoing. Seven percent of the responding whistleblowers reported serious financial irregularities, which is the main focus of this article.

The wrongdoer was predominantly a colleague in Bjørkelo et al.'s (2011) study, and the wrongdoing was most often instantly stopped or reduced. Whistleblowers reported that wrongdoers received mixed reactions including just as much "no reaction" as "reprimand".

Whistleblowers reported to be met with both high levels of "no response" and low levels of "reward". Nothing happened to most of them. However, more whistleblowers than non-whistleblowers reported to be exposed to workplace bullying.

Bjørkelo et al.'s (2011) results in Norway might be compared to the UK, where Jones (2016) found that despite organizations encouraging employees to speak up about misconduct, organizations struggle to engage their staff to do so. Overall, it seems that Norway has a better record of responding to and protecting whistleblowers.

7. Two Whistleblowers

The two whistleblowers are compared in Tables 1 and 2. A and B blew the whistle independent of each other. Whistleblower A is 52 years old, and he has been employed in Grimstad municipality for 7 years. Whistleblower B is 61 years, and he has been employed in the municipality for 20 years. They both hired defense attorneys when they experienced reprisals.

Whistleblower A told in the interview that he has a reputation of being a critical finance manager.

He has always been open-minded when detecting misconduct. Within the health and care sector, there have been several negative deviations earlier. He considers himself to be an open and skilled person who tries to get hold of episodes as soon as they occur. His goal is to improve attitudes and routines. He reacts strongly to abuse of privileged positions.

Table 1.

Comparison of whistleblowers in Grimstad municipality (1:2)

Issue	Whistleblower A	Whistleblower B	Comparison
Position in organization	Chief Financial Officer (CFO) in Grimstad municipality.	Special advisor to the councilor in Grimstad municipality.	At levels 3 (A) and 2 (B) in the hierarchy respectively.
Contents of warning	Assistant municipal manager for health and care services favors her sister-in-law as provider of health services without proper procurement process and incapacity.	Illegal direct purchases of NOK 50-100 million from 2012 to 2016, possibly corruption.	B formulates more specific allegations than A.
Point in time	April 2016.	February 2017. (Notice earlier).	More specific warning later by both A and B.
Recipients of warning	Acting councilor and municipal manager who is the CFO's superior.	All members of municipal council. (Notice to a few).	B distributed more widely than A.
Reaction to warning	First, no reaction, denied receipt. Normal management. Next, auditing report confirms warning.	First, ignorance and rejection. Next, whistleblowing letter not processed. Then, public harassment.	Public support for B after media attention.
Media first time	December 2016.	February 2017.	B more open to media than A.
Reprisals from employer	Disregard, deprived responsibility for work tasks, called on the carpet, hung out in report.	Lost assignments, criticized publicly by the mayor, breach of confidentiality.	Tougher treatment of B than A.
Defense lawyer response	Criticism of internal investigation, legal process, lack of independence, and lack of objectivity. Claim for retaliation.	Claim for redemption of NOK 300.000 and possible compensation claim in the future.	B sued his employer, A did not so far.
Status for	Sick leave because of	Sick leave because of	B does some

whistleblower June 2017	reprisals.	reprisals.	municipality work, A does not.

Table 2.

Comparison of whistleblowers in Grimstad municipality (2:2)

Issue	Whistleblower A	Whistleblower B	Comparison
Silence is golden?	Must raise voice when misconduct occurs in the organization.	Never considered not to blow the whistle	No regrets and would both do it again.
Blown the whistle before?	No, but in the case of more unreasonable decisions.	As children's ombudsman blew the whistle in 2003.	B more exposed than A.
Conspiracy theory?	Financial motive when sister-in-law gets contracts for services not required. Link between religious leaders in the community.	Link between health services procurement and foreign aid in Africa. Link between religious leaders in the community.	Agree on links to religious organizations involved in Africa mission.
Who are friends?	Some politicians, the audit, employees who have been taken over.	Inhabitants, media, some politicians, and a very few colleagues.	Similar friends.
Who are enemies?	Executives, to whom the criticism is addressed, police management, as well as administrative senior personnel.	Previous and current political and bureaucratic top level people in the municipality.	Similar enemies.
Trade union support?	No, union leaders loyal to executive management rather than members.	Some support from local union.	B more independent of union leaders than A.
Professional information handling?	No, information about whistleblower leaked in the town hall.	More open to information sharing.	A more discomfort at public attention than B.

When A blew the whistle, he experienced ignorance and lack of responsibility and accountability from his superiors. When the BDO (2016) report became publicly available, his name was often mentioned in a negative context. In January 2017, he contacted a lawyer and claimed retaliation (Eriksen, 2017), and provided several examples of reprisals. He then experienced strong expulsion from union officials, as well as employees and managers. He felt he was stabbed in the back. Many looked away, went another way and did not say hello.

When whistleblower B emerged, whistleblower A experienced that the pressure on himself was reduced. Instead, he was completely ignored. After a while on sick leave, he was called in on the carpet to be told that his CFO position was to disappear because of reorganization.

Whistleblower A expressed his frustration in an e-mail saying (Kluge, 2017: 7):

"I feel that I am banned from the inter-municipal ERP project. Throughout the autumn, I have asked the local executive of business management if it would be appropriate for me to participate. This is because ERP is the core system of my area of responsibility. The system includes accounting, reporting, and budgeting".

In the whistleblowing case A, Grimstad's law firm partner concluded that no retaliation had occurred (Kluge, 2017: 66):

"Based on our investigations, it is our opinion that the chief financial officer has not been subject to retaliation on the basis of his notice".

The 66-pages report by Kluge (2017) discusses a series of incidents where A was treated badly, but each episode does not in itself represent retaliation according to the law firm. However taken together, both the number of incidents and the kind of incidents seem to represent retaliation and reprisals from his superiors (Olsen, 2017).

Whistleblower A is convinced that retaliation occurred because of his statements in the BDO (2016) investigation report on health service purchases. In the report, A describes the climate for negative expressions and alerts as really bad in Grimstad municipality:

Whistleblower B was much more exposed in the media, and some quotes illustrate his attitude (Skår and Andersen, 2017):

"It is absolutely unacceptable to leave the case".

He is called whistleblower, but actually he just did his job. He simply told about illegal purchases in Grimstad municipality.

He became aware of the misconduct in the spring of 2016. He realized that there were direct acquisitions without framework agreements. These should be in the order of one hundred million Norwegian kroner.

He also discovered that the malpractice had been going on for several years, and that there were more people in the municipality who knew about it. Despite that, he was the first to take action, as far as he knew at the time.

"For my part, I reacted strongly that no one had informed the Control Committee in a proper manner. This is a very serious violation of very basic standards", he says.

B blew the whistle twice concerning illegal procurement of health care services. He did it first time to the chairman of the control committee and to the leader of the auditing service in April 2016. That started the case rolling. They promised confidentiality. But they did not keep their promise. The second time was open whistleblowing to the entire municipality council.

B has been employed in Grimstad municipality for 27 years. He perceives retaliation from both the councilor and the mayor of the town (Eriksen, 2017).

The police showed little interest neither in the case of possible law violation in terms of corruption at public procurement or in the case of possible law violations by reprisals and retaliation (Berg, 2017).

8. Discussion

This article explores the experiences of two whistleblowers in the context of a municipality. Exploring the individual and contextual drivers of unethical behavior is an important line of inquiry within occupational and organizational psychology, and case studies can be helpful in providing new insights.

An interesting observation in the Grimstad case is that very many people have left their positions in the municipality in recent years. For example, one of the suspects, the deputy manager for health and care, whose sister-in-law is running the health care businesses, resigned in June 2017 to take on a similar position in a neighboring municipality. It seemed that many saw a potential crisis coming if the Control Committee with the help of an external investigator would get to the bottom of the health service procurement case and the whistleblower handling case.

The whistleblowers received massive support in the community as local newspapers (e.g., Berg, 2016, 2017; Karlsen, 2017) presented more facts about their case. For example, Schieldrop (2017: 18) expressed his support by stating that the whistleblowers deserve respect:

"Whistleblowers are to me honorary men who dare stand up and say hello, here is something that is not correct, something that must and should withstand the light of day".

In July 2017, another act of retaliation occurred from the councilman on whistleblower A. The councilman presented to him an organization map where he was no longer included (Ellingsen, 2017; Eriksen, 2017).

The experience of whistleblowers A and B can be discussed in terms of general findings from research on whistleblowing in local government in Norway. Skivenes and Trygstad (2016) conducted such an empirical study of contact patterns and whistleblowing in 20 Norwegian municipalities. They found that a lower degree of contact between politicians and administrative employees is correlated with negative perceptions of whistleblowing and destructive handling of wrongdoing reports by the politicians.

Skivenes and Trygstad (2016) applied institutional theory as a platform to understand how tensions between and within regulative environments in local governments can affect the contact patterns between politicians and employees in the municipality. The two main findings of their study are that contact between politicians and administrative employees is common and that the degree of contact between politicians and administrative employees is positively correlated with politicians who take action to address whistleblowing cases.

In the Grimstad case, there seems to be a substantial extent of contact between politicians and administrative employees. Nevertheless, the whistleblowing from A and B has not really been addressed. One reason might be that the communication challenge cannot be found between administration and politics, but rather within the administration itself.

There are several avenues for future research. While there is a depth that the presented Grimstad case offers, including the use of interviews and text documents from our inquiry, the focus on two cases of individual whistleblowers in one particular setting provides only a narrow and limited account. Next, there is a need to embed and contribute to psychological theory. There are a number of research studies on unethical behavior, and they should be included in future research. Studies by Morrison (2014) and Trevino et al. (2014) are two examples.

9. Conclusion

Characteristics and experiences of whistleblowers is an important field of research for work and organizational psychology. Detection and prevention of misconduct and crime is dependent on people internally who are not afraid to speak up and tell about their observations. This article has presented two whistleblowers who – despite perceived retaliation and reprisals – are willing to do it again. They simply define it as part of their job.

This article discussed an example of how local workplace and organizational cultures as well as local societal cultures (family bonds, religious bonds) are often stronger than, and therefore overpowering of legal and policy frameworks. The example emphasized suspicion of white-collar crime, as the whistleblowers pointed upwards in the organization concerning misconduct and potential financial crime. While Norway has been traditionally regarded as a country that is more positively disposed towards whistleblowers than some other countries, the Grimstad case illustrates that also Norway may have a long way to go.

It is obviously too soon to reach final conclusions, given that some aspects of the case are still to be determined. For example, neither internal e-mail investigation nor police investigation is decided at this point in time. It may be that it will be easier to make sense of all of this when some of the remaining issues have been resolved. However, it is interesting and relevant to present research of a phenomenon where the final outcome is not known. It is important that this research is not influential or even prejudicial to ongoing investigations, as everyone is innocent until the opposite is convincingly proven.

References

BDO (2016). *Rapport til kontrollutvalget. Undersøkelse om kjøp av helsetjenester i Grimstad kommune (Report to the control committee. Review of health services procurement in Grimstad municipality)*, auditing firm BDO, Oslo, Norway.

Berg, P.Y. (2016). Fikk nei til dypere graving i helsekjøpssaken (Got no to dig deeper into the health care case), local daily newspaper *Agderposten*, www.agderposten.no, published December 23.

Berg, P.Y. (2017). Ber politiet etterforske (Asks police to investigate), local Norwegian newspaper *Agderposten*, Tuesday, July 4, page 13.

Bjørkelo, B., Einarsen, S., Nielsen, M.B. and Matthiesen, S.B. (2011). Silence is golden? Characteristics and experiences of self-reported whistleblowers, *European Journal of Work and Organizational Psychology*, 20 (2), 206-238.

Brooks, G. and Button, M. (2011). The police and fraud investigation and the case for a nationalized solution in the United Kingdom, *The Police Journal*, 84, 305-319.

Button, M. and Gee, J. (2013). *Countering Fraud for Competitive Advantage – The Professional Approach to Reducing the Last Great Hidden Cost*, Chichester, UK: Wiley & Sons.

Button, M., Frimpong, K., Smith, G. and Johnston, L. (2007). Professionalizing counter fraud specialists in the UK: assessing progress and recommendations for reform, *Crime Prevention and Community Safety*, 9, 92-101.

Creswell, J.W. (2003). *Research Design. Qualitative, Quantitative, and Mixed Methods Approaches*, 2nd edition, Sage Publications, California: Thousand Oaks.

Ellingsen, T. (2017). –Varsler risikerer å bli degradert (Whistleblower risks being degraded), daily Norwegian newspaper *Agderposten*, Tuesday, July 25, pages 10-11.

Eriksen, B. (2017). Ordfører e-post eskalerer konflikten (Mayor's email escalates municipality conflict), local daily newspaper *Agderposten*, Saturday, September 9, page 25.

Gottschalk, P. (2016). Private policing of financial crime: Key issues in the investigation business in Norway, *European Journal of Policing Studies*, 3 (3), 292-314.

Gottschalk, P. (2017). Convenience in white-collar crime: Introducing a core concept, *Deviant Behavior*, 38 (5), 605-619.

Gottschalk, P. and Smith, C. (2016). Detection of white-collar corruption in public procurement in Norway: The role of whistleblowers, *International Journal of Procurement Management*, 9 (4), 427-443.

Jones, A. (2016). The Role of Employee Whistleblowing and Raising Concerns in an Organizational Learning Culture – Elusive and Laudable? *International Journal of Health Policy and Management*, 5 (1), 67-69.

Karlsen, K. (2017). Ulike meninger om rådmannen bør permitteres (Differing opinions whether councilwomen should leave), daily local newspaper *Grimstad Adressetidende*, Saturday, June 24, page 11.

Kluge (2017). *Undersøkelse av varsling og påstand om gjengjeldelse (Examination of warning and claim for retaliation)*, law firm Kluge, Oslo, May 5.

Lee, F. og Robinson, R.J. (2000). An Attributional Analysis of Social Accounts: Implications of Playing the Blame Game, *Journal of Applied Social Psychology*, 30 (9), 1853-1879.

McClelland, P.L., Liang, X. and Barker, V.L. (2010). CEO Commitment to the Status Quo: Replication and Extension Using Content Analysis, *Journal of Management*, 36 (5), 1251-1277.

Morrison, E.W. (2014). Employee voice and silence, *Annual Review of Organizational Psychology and Organizational Behavior*, 1 (1), 173-197.

Mpho, B. (2017). Whistleblowing: What do contemporary ethical theories say? *Studies in Business and Economics*, 12 (1), 19-28.

Nesti, L. (2014). The 2010 "Agreement on mutual enforcement of debarments decisions" and its impact for the fight against fraud and corruption in public procurement, *Journal of Public Procurement*, 14 (1), 62-95.

Olsen, M. (2017). *Grimstad kommune – Helge Moen, Undersøkelse av varsling m.m., (Grimstad municipality – Investigation into whistleblowing),* Advokatfirma Hald & Co. Arendal, Norway.

Patrucco, A.S., Luzzini, D. and Ronchi, S. (2017). Research perspectives on public procurement: Content analysis of 14 years of publications in the Journal of Public Procurement, *Journal of Public Procurement*, 16 (2), 229-269.

Pittroff, E. (2014). Whistle-Blowing Systems and Legitimacy Theory: A Study of Motivation to Implement Whistle-Blowing Systems in German Organizations, *Journal of Business Ethics*, 124, 399-412.

Rothwell, G.R. and Baldwin, J.N. (2007). Ethical Climate Theory, Whistle-blowing, and the Code of Silence in Police Agencies in the State of Georgia, *Journal of Business Ethics*, 70, 341-361.

Schieldrop, E. (2017). Varslerne fortjener respekt og integritet (The whistleblowers deserve respect and integrity), local Norwegian daily newspaper *Agderposten*, Saturday, July 15, page 18.

Schneider, S. (2006). Privatizing Economic Crime Enforcement: Exploring the Role of Private Sector Investigative Agencies in Combating Money Laundering, *Policing & Society*, 16 (3), 285-312.

Skivenes, M. and Trygstad, S.C. (2016). Whistleblowing in Local Government: An Empirical Study of Contact Patterns and Whistleblowing in 20 Norwegian Municipalities, *Scandinavian Political Studies*, 39 (3), 264-289.

Skår, K.L. and Andersen, E.W. (2017). –Det er helt uaktuelt å la saken ligge (It is absolutely unacceptable to leave the case), public Norwegian broadcasing *NRK*, www.nrk.no, published February 14.

Strand, M.E. (2017). 3 av 4 mistenker korrupsjon i kommunen sin (3 out of 4 suspect corruption in their municipality), daily Norwegian newspaper *Agderposten*, Friday, August 18, pages 8-9.

Sundström, M. and Radon, A. (2015). Utilizing the concept of convenience as a business opportunity in emerging markets, *Organizations and Markets in Emerging Economies*, 6 (2), 7-21.

Sutherland, E.H. (1939). White-collar criminality, *American Sociological Review*, 5: 1-12.

Sutherland, E.H. (1949). *White-Collar Crime*, Holt, Rinehart and Winston Publishing, NY: New York.

Sutherland, E.H. (1983). *White Collar Crime – The Uncut Version*, New Haven, CT: Yale University Press.

Trevino, L.K., den Nieuwenboer, N.A. and Kish-Gephart, J.J. (2014). (Un)ethical behavior in organizations, *Annual Review of Psychology*, 65, 635-660.

Uhl-Bien, M. and Carsten, M.K. (2007). Being Ethical When the Boss is Not, *Organizational Dynamics*, 36 (2), 187-201.

Williams, J.W. (2005). Governability Matters: The Private Policing of Economic Crime and the Challenge of Democratic Governance, *Policing & Society*, 15 (2), 187-211.

Yin, R.K. (2003). *Case Study Research. Design and Methods,* 3rd edition, Sage Publications, California: Thousand Oaks.

Journal of International Doctoral Research (JIDR)

Counsellors' Need of Social Support

Lars Glasø [a]

Tina Løkke Vie[b]

Stig Berge Matthiesen[a]

[a] BI Norwegian Business School, Oslo, Norway

[b] Førde Health Trust, Norway

ABSTRACT

The present study investigates the impact of social support on mental health among Norwegian counsellors. Data were collected by means of anonymous self-report questionnaires addressing central aspects of the counsellors' job, health and well-being. The results show that leader support act as a strong predictor of counsellors' mental health compared to other sources of social support, such as co-worker support, family support and friend support. Furthermore, the results indicate that leader support moderates and has a stress-preventing effect on the relationship between perceived stress and mental health. Thus, the findings suggest that leader support is an important factor likely to influence the health of counsellors.

Key Words: *Leadership, counsellors, social support, strain, mental health.*

Introduction

Theoretically, work-related health outcomes have been explained by the stressor-strain relationship (Beehr, 1995; Harris & Kackmar, 2005), where physical or psychosocial work characteristics are viewed as predictors to stress reactions and strains. Although stress reactions may serve an adaptive function e.g., "eustress" (Simmons & Nelson, 2001), considerable research has shown that certain job stressors can elicit physical and psychological stress responses which over time can result in physical and psychological strain, including cardiovascular disease, high blood pressure, anxiety and depression (Cartwright, 2010; Kaufmann & Beehr, 1986; Lazarus & Folkman, 1984; Simmons & Nelson, 2001).

One variable thought to influence individual strain reactions is social support (Ganstner, Fusilier & Mayes, 1986; Viswesvaran, Sanches & Fisher, 1999). Social support is defined as the availability of helping relationships and the quality of those relationships (Leavy, 1983). While the stress process involves a multitude of influential factors, including work environment and personal characteristics, the degree of social support that individuals receive has been recognized as a highly relevant "buffer" protecting individuals from the pathological consequences of stressful experiences (Cohen & Wills, 1985). From a social support perspective, leaders represent an important resource likely to influence their subordinates' health, as leaders' behaviour seems to play an important role regarding the degree to which a work setting is perceived as 'supportive' (House, 1981; Thanacoody, Bartram & Casimir, 2009).

Counsellors constitute a special work group. Using therapeutic techniques as their tools and the consultation room as their arena, their job is to provide care to others in need of support and guidance. But then the questions arise: Where do counsellors themselves find social support? Does it come from their superiors or elsewhere? The aim of the present study is to examine the role of social support as it is experienced by a nationally representative group of Norwegian psychologists. The importance of such support will be compared with other types of support from co-workers, family and friends. Mental health will comprise the outcome measure.

In Norway most psychologists work as counsellors or therapists. As such, they are daily confronted with intense emotions and the troublesome conflicts of other people, including suicide threats, aggressive hostility, psychotic behavior, and criminality (Deutsch, 1984). However, there are also other aspects of the profession that may contribute to a counsellor's distress. According to Baker (2003), achievement, career development, an increased standard of living, upward mobility, status, and prestige all come at a price in terms of amount of work, pressure and health-related strain. Based on the nature of their work, counsellors represent an important group for study with regard to stress reduction. For example, a review of studies of UK clinical psychologists suggests that the majority find their work highly demanding, and up to 40% experience high levels of distress (Hannigan et al., 2004). In a qualitative study, Rønnestad and Skovholt (2003) interviewed 100 American counselors/therapists at different experience levels. Overall, as many as 1/3 of therapists reported stressful involvement with their clients (see also Orlinsky & Rønnestad, 2005). Accordingly, studies have shown that psychologists report health-related strains such as burnout (Ackerley, Burnell, Holder & Kardek, 1988; Farber, 1990; Guy, Poelstra & Stark, 1989; Rupert & Morgan, 2005), fatigue, irritability, disillusionment, self-doubt (Mahoney, 1997), exhaustion, depression and vicarious traumatization (Smith & Moss, 2009). Today, there is academic consensus that therapy and counselling is a major mediator of burnout for psychologists (Nissen-Lie, Monsen, Ulleberg & Rønnestad, 2013; Thériault & Gazzola, 2005).

Stressful work conditions may not only affect the counsellors themselves, but can also have negative effects on patient care, highlighting the need to identify important factors that can alleviate the potential strains experienced by this group of professionals (Smith & Moss, 2009). Yet, according to Rupert and Morgan (2005), research regarding counsellors has been too narrow and has consisted primarily of investigations of the stress of psychotherapeutic work as correlates of burnout. Research on other mental health variables is still limited, and research thus far basically has involved surveys that have included small samples of counsellors (Bearse, McMinn, Seegobin & Free, 2013).

As outlined above, social support can be considered as a potential resource likely to influence individuals' strain reactions. More specifically, social support may take the form of emotional support - provision of empathy, love and caring; instrumental support - provision of material goods and services; informational support - provision of suggestions and advice; and appraisal support - provision of information that is helpful for self-evaluation purposes (House, 1981). Yet the types of social support have not always been clearly distinguished. Some researchers have focused only on one type of support (e.g., Kickul & Posig, 2001), while others have combined separate measures of different types of social support into a single index, assuming that the various aspects of social support are highly interrelated, e.g., offering informational support often concurrently implies giving affective support, in addition to direct aid (Frese, 1999).

It has been common to distinguish between work-related and non-work-related sources of social support. Work-related sources of social support refer to social support from leaders and coworkers, whereas non-work-related sources refer to extra-organizational sources, such as spouse, family and friends (van Daalen, Sanders & Willemsen, 2005). According to Beehr (1985), work-related stress is most effectively managed by work-related sources of support, since the stress response occurs in the context of the stressful situation (see also Barling, Bluen & Fain, 1987; Viswesvaran, Sanches & Fisher, 1999). In this respect leaders hold a central position being salient persons in an individual's work context, and therefore are likely to exert a direct influence on subordinates' behavior (Kozlowski & Doherty, 1989; O'disroll & Beehr, 1994). Consistent with this view, the leadership literature provides ample evidence that subordinates are strongly influenced by leader behavior, regardless of whether that behavior is perceived as good or bad (Glasø, Skogstad, Notelaers & Einarsen, 2017).

Leader behavior such as consideration, support, and empowerment have been related to increased psychological well-being (Amundsen & Martinsen, 2014; Gottfredson & Aquinis, 2017; Ng, 2017), less perceived stress (Harris & Kackmar, 2006) and less burnout among employees (Huang, Chan, Lam, & Nan, 2010). Conversely, unsupportive leader behaviors such as abusive supervision (Tepper, 2000), Laissez faire leadership (Skogstad, Hetland, Glasø & Einarsen, 2014) and lack of interactional justice (Kelloway, Sivanthan, Francis & Barling, 2004), have been related to high levels of stress and negative health outcomes. Yet some studies have shown that other non-work-related sources of support may be more effective than workplace support in alleviating the effects of work-related strain. For example, in a study of teachers, Greenglass, Fiksenbaum and Burke (1994) found that family support was more effective than workplace support in easing the effects of work stress on burnout. Moreover, in a study of 211 traffic enforcement agents, Baruch-Feldman et al., (2002) found that family support was more closely associated with burnout than with satisfaction or with productivity, whereas immediate supervisor support was related to satisfaction and productivity but not to burnout. Thus, despite abundant evidence of the beneficial effects of social support in general, it is still unclear as to what extent social support from leaders influences subordinates' health, as compared to other sources of social support.

Further, it is unclear *how* social support from leaders may influence the health of employees. In the mainstream literature, different theoretical models of how social support affects the stressor–strain relationship have been suggested. According to Dormann and Zapf (1999), the majority of the social support studies investigate one of the following hypotheses: (1) *the direct (main) effect*, assuming that social support has a direct positive impact on health, e.g., the more support people receive, the less likely symptoms of mental or physical ill-health will appear, (2) *the moderating (interaction) effect* also known as the buffering effect, assuming that social support moderates the relationship between stressors and strains, i.e., social support works as a buffer and prevents stressors from developing their impact on strain, meaning that there is a strong stressor-strain relationship when support is low, and a weak or no stressor-strain relationship when support is high, (3) *the indirect (mediating) effect*, assuming that social support reduces the strength of the stressor and subsequently reduces the probability of ill-health, indicating that social support may have a stress-preventive effect by influencing the stress perception, which again will influence health, and thus act as a mediator between leader support and health outcomes.

The hypotheses presented above have been separately tested in several studies. For instance, research has found that leader support may have a direct effect on subordinates' health in terms of burnout (Graham & Witteloostuijn, 2010), affective and somatic outcomes (Ganster et al., 1986), whereas a study by Lee (2011) has provided evidence that leader support, in terms of leader-member-exchange (LMX) (Graen & Uhl-Bien, 1995; Gottfredson & Aquinis, 2017) may moderate the stressor-strain relationship. Furthermore, Thomas and Lankau (2009) found that supportive leader behavior minimizes emotional exhaustion through increased socialization and decreased role stress. On the other hand, Dormann and Zapf (1999) did not find any main effect of leader support on depression in a longitudinal study among Germany citizens, yet they did find a moderating effect. However, the picture is blurred, as there are also studies that do not support the notion of a moderator effect of leader support on mental health, only the existence of a main effect (e.g., Ganster et al., 1986).

The inconclusive findings regarding leader support processes may be due to different contexts, designs and operationalizations of the concepts of stress and support. In line with this, van der Doef and Maes (1999) argue for a more occupation-specific approach, suggesting that prior research regarding the stressor-strain relationship largely ignores the impact of the job situation itself. Using more job-specific measurements for occupational groups may enable a more specific understanding, and would accordingly lead to the development of more appropriate interventions in the workplace to improve employees' health (Collins, Hislop & Cartwright, 2016; Glasø, Bele, Nielsen, & Einarsen, 2011; Richardsen & Martinussen, 2007).

Based on these arguments, the purpose of the present study is to investigate the need of social support to a large sample of counsellors in Norway. One aim is to examine to what extent social support from leaders as compared to other sources of social support influences the counsellors' strain reactions in terms of mental health. Given the unique demands and professional challenges involved in a counsellor's work, and that stress coping occurs in the context of the stressful situation (Beehr, 1985), it seems plausible that work-related stress is effectively dealt with by work-related sources of support, and in particular social support from leaders. Although the job-autonomy of many counsellors seems to be high as they provide care on a one-to-one basis, many also work in team-based constellations, as well as in professional-based bureaucracies (e.g., hospitals and school systems), where the work is highly regulated and the leader may represent a difference with regard to their perceived stressors at work. Further, given the leaders' role in defining and influencing an environment in which employees can thrive and feel worthy (Skakon, Nielsen, Borg, & Guzman, 2010), we assume that leaders would be an important source of social support, and, according to the direct effect hypothesis (Dormann & Zapf, 1999) will have a direct influence on the mental health of counsellors. To empirically investigate this assumption, we will test the following hypothesis:

> H1: *Leader support will significantly improve the prediction of mental health among counsellors.*

Further, on the basis of the theoretical models of *how* social support may affect the stressor–strain relationship (see Dormann & Zapf, 1999), we hypothesize that leadership support not only has a direct influence on health, but will also act as a moderator in the stressor-strain relationship. This leads to the next hypothesis:

H2: *Leader support moderates the relationship between perceived stress and mental health among counsellors.*

Finally, while H2 proposes that leader support intervenes after stress perception and exerts its effect by reducing the severity of the stress response, thus avoiding or moderating risks to health, we also hypothesize that leader support may indirectly influence the probability of ill-health through the mechanism of stress-perception. This means that leader support directly influences perceived stress and subsequently the probability of ill-health, meaning that social support has a stress-preventive effect. This will be tested in the following hypothesis:

H3: *The relationship between leader support and counsellors' mental health is mediated by perceived stress.*

The theoretical model that captures H1-H3 is presented in figure 1.

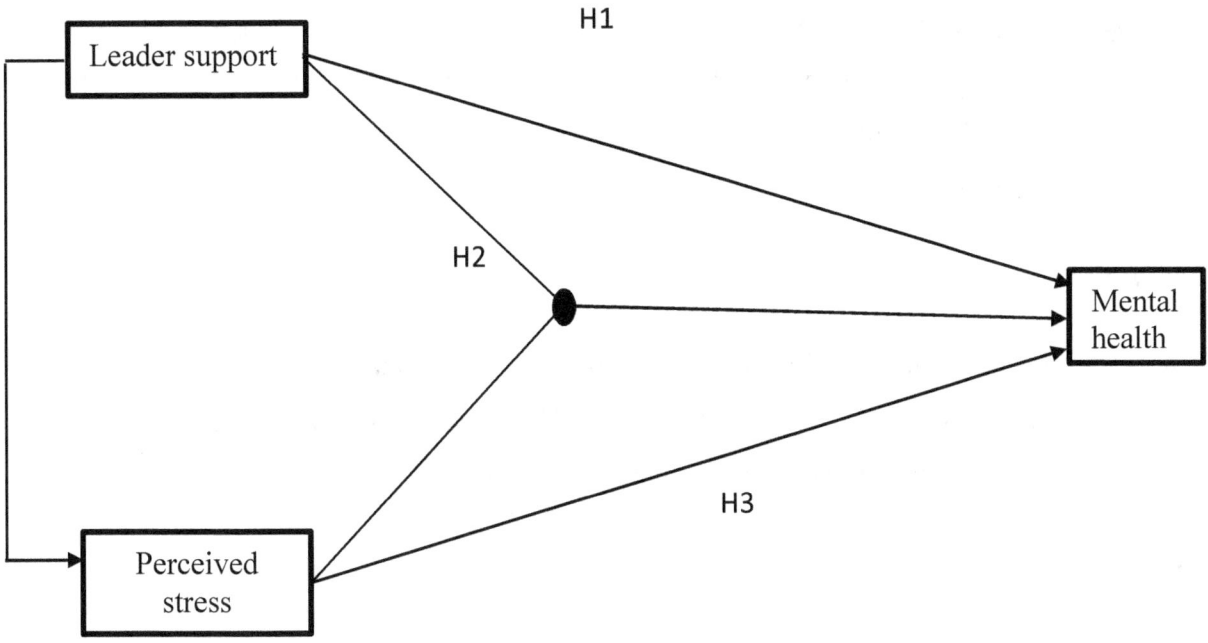

Figure 1: Theoretical model: The link between leader support, perceived stress and mental health among counsellors.

Method

Sample

Counsellors may come from many different professional backgrounds. In this study we have chosen an occupation specific approach, by collecting data from one specific group of counsellors, namely psychologists. Data was collected by means of anonymous self-report questionnaires distributed to 2,160 Norwegian psychologists. In Norway, the majority of psychologists work in a clinical setting, practicing counselling and therapy. The sample included 1,402 respondents (56.1% male and 43.9% female), yielding an overall response rate of 65%. The mean age of the sample was 41 years ($SD = 8.17$), ranging from 26 to 72 years. Among the respondents, 69.5% worked full-time, 43.5% had leadership responsibility (60.2% male and 53.3% female; mean age leaders 42 years ($SD=8,2$), non-leaders 40 ($SD=7,8$)). Average job tenure was 11 years, 10.2% of the respondents reported being a chief psychologist while 48 % were specialists approved by the Norwegian Psychological Association. As much as 43% worked in organizations with 1-10 employees, while 20% were employed at institutions with more than 100 employees. Of the respondents, 82.4% had children, 85.5% were married or cohabitants, while 14.5% lived alone.

Procedure

Data were collected by the use of the survey method. The questionnaires were distributed by post by the Norwegian Psychological Association (NPF). The response rate was good, approximately 65 % of those who got the questionnaire by mail responded.

Questionnaire

Demographic information constituted the first part of the questionnaire. Participants were asked to report their age, gender, number of subordinates, current employment status, civil status, and number of children.

Perceived social support. Perceived social support was measured by three items based on House (1981). The respondents were asked how much (1) practical support, (2) emotional support, and (3) constructive feedback they get from six different groups of people: leaders, co-workers within the same profession, co-workers from another profession, union representatives, friends, and family. All six measures of perceived social support had satisfactory internal consistencies. Chronbach's alphas were: .84 (leader support), .82 (co-worker, same profession), .80 (co-worker, another profession), .81 (union representatives), .77 (family), and .77 (friends), respectively. The respondents were asked to rate their perceived level of support by means of four possible alternatives; "not at all", "a little", "a lot" and "very much".

Stress was measured by the Health Professions Stress Inventory (HPSI) (Wolfgang, 1988). The HPSI assesses both level and source of perceived stress of health professionals actively engaged in clinical practice. The measure contains 30 generally stressful situations gleaned from the literature, such as 'handling difficult clients'. Respondents are asked to identify how often they experience the particular situations using a 5-point Likert scale of "never", "seldom", "sometimes", "often" and "very often". In the present study, the HPSI had a satisfactory internal consistency, with Cronbach's alpha being .87.

Mental health was measured by 20 items from the General Health Questionnaire (GHQ; Goldberg, 1978), which is a measure of common mental health problems/domains, such as anxiety and depression. The GHQ was designed to be used as a screening instrument to identify psychological distress and short-term changes in mental health in community and health care settings (Goldberg & Williams, 1988; Penninkilampi-Kerola, Miettunen & Ebeling, 2006). The respondents were asked to indicate how often they had experienced different health conditions over the last two weeks. Examples of some items include: 'Have you found everything getting on top of you?'; 'Have you been getting scared or panicky for no good reason?' and 'Have you been getting edgy and bad tempered?'. Each item is accompanied by four possible responses, typically being 'not at all', 'no more than usual', 'rather more than usual' and 'much more than usual'. The mental health variable used in the analyses is a total sum score of all stressful situations measured in the GHQ. In the present study, the GHQ had a satisfactory internal consistency, with Cronbach's alpha being .91.

Statistics

Statistical analyses were conducted using the IBM Statistical Package for Social Sciences (SPSS) 19. Frequency, reliability and correlation analyses were employed on all the study's variables, and hierarchical regression analyses were conducted in order to investigate the hypotheses. The mediator and moderator analyses were performed by steps recommended by Baron and Kenny (1986). The Sobel test for significance of indirect effects was used to test the possible indirect effect of leader support (http://quantpsy.org/sobel/sobel.htm). The level of significance was set to .05.

Results

The means, standard deviations, and correlations (Pearson's *r*) among the study's variables, including age and gender, are shown in Table 1. Age was related to gender, perceived stress, leader support, and social support from co-workers from another profession. Gender was related to friend support and perceived stress. The sources of social support were positively related to one another, with r's varying between .12 and .42. Most sources of social support were related to perceived stress and mental health with the exception of social support from union representatives. Leader support showed the strongest correlation with mental health, as compared to the other sources of social support. Perceived stress and mental health correlated with one another.

Table 1.

Means, standard deviations, and correlations for the measured variables

Variables	1	2	3	4	5	6	7	8	9	10
1. Age	–									
2. Gender	-.07**	–								
3. Leader support	-.08**	-.06	–							
4. Co-worker [a] support	.02	.02	.36**	–						
5. Co-worker [b] support	.06*	.01	.31**	.34**	–					
6. Representative support	.06	-.02	.24**	.38**	.24**	–				
7. Family support	.05	-.03	.12**	.18**	.18**	.19**	–			
8. Friend support	.05	.18**	.14**	.24**	.21**	.25**	.42**	–		
9. Perceived stress	-.09**	.06*	-.29**	-.23**	-.13**	-.04	-.08*	-.08**	–	
10. Mental health	.01	.01	-.24**	-.17**	-.11**	-.05	-.16**	-.07*	.32**	–
M	41.04	1.44	2.51	2.72	2.64	1.68	2.83	2.41	2.49	1.90
SD	8.17	0.50	0.78	0.72	0.68	0.67	0.75	0.74	0.41	0.35

Note. N= 980-1380. Gender: 1 = male, 2 = female. [a]co-worker from same profession, [b]co-worker from another profession. ** *p*<.01; * *p*<.05, two-tailed.

Table 2 shows the results of the regression analyses for different sources of social support as predictors of mental health, after controlling for age and gender. None of the control variables were significant predictors of health outcomes (step 1), while inclusion of the social support variables (step 2) resulted in a significant increase of the explained variance ($R^2 = .04$, $p < .001$). Moreover, inclusion of the leader support variable (step 3) resulted in a significant increase of the explained variance ($R^2 = .04$, $p < .001$), controlled for the other social support variables. For the linear effect, leader support acted as the strongest predictor of mental health ($\beta = .21$, $p < .001$) as compared to the other sources of support, where only support from co-workers from the same profession ($\beta = .15$; $p < .01$), other profession ($\beta = .07$; $p < .05$) and family ($\beta = .09$; $p < .01$) yielded significant contributions. Thus, the results support H1, that leader support has the strongest and an independent direct influence on mental health as compared to other sources of social support.

Table 2.

Hierarchical multiple regression analyses predicting mental health from leader support, as compared to other sources of support.

			Mental health	
	Predictor	ß	R^2	ΔR^2
Step 1			.00	
	Age	-.01		
	Gender	-.00		
Step 2			.04***	.04***
	Co-worker support	.15**		
	Co-worker[b] support	.07*		
	Representative support	-.02		
	Family support	.09**		
	Friend support	-.03		
Step 3			.08***	.04***
	Leader support	.21***		

Note. [b]co-worker from another profession, *** $p<.001$; ** $p<.01$; * $p<.05$, two-tailed. listwise, N= 957.

Multiple regression analyses were employed in order to examine whether leader support acts as a moderator on the relationship between perceived stress and mental health (see Table 3). For the linear effect, perceived stress and leader support explained 12 % of the variance in health outcomes. Both perceived stress ($\beta = .27$; $p < .001$) and leader support ($\beta = -.16$; $p < .001$) yielded significant contributions. Further, the interaction-term made a significant contribution to the explained variance (β = -.08; p <.05), resulting in a small but significant increase in the explained variance (R^2 = .01, p < .05). Thus, in support of H2 leader support was found to moderate the relationship between perceived stress and mental health.

Table 3.

Hierarchical multiple regression testing the moderating role of leader support on the relationship between perceived stress and mental health

| | | Mental health | |
Predictor	ß	R^2	ΔR^2
Step 1		.12***	
Perceived stress	.27***		
Leader support	-.16***		
Step 2		.13***	.01*
Perceived stress	.25***		
Leader support	-.16***		
Perceived stress x Leader support	-.08*		

Note. *** p<.001; ** p<.01; * p<.05, two-tailed, N=792.

To test for mediation (or whether leader support influences employees' stress perception, which again will influence their health), multiple regression analysis was utilized. According to Baron and Kenny (1986), mediation exists if the following criteria are met: (a) Leader support should significantly predict perceived stress and mental health, (b) perceived stress should significantly predict mental health, and (c) the effect of leader support on health should disappear or at least be reduced when perceived stress is added to the equation. These conditions are met in the present study. Leader support contributed significantly to the explained variance in mental health (β = -.24; p <.001). Further, perceived stress contributed significantly to a reduction in the effect of leader support on mental health (from β = -.24; p <.001 to β = -.16; p <.001). The Sobel test revealed that the mediating effect of perceived stress was significant (p <.001). This result supports H3 that the relationship between leader support and mental health is mediated by perceived stress. The leader support predictor remained significant, however, indicating stress to be a partial mediator between leader support and mental health.

Discussion

The results of the present study show that leader support is related to the mental health of Norwegian counsellors. With regard to the direct effect, leader support was found to be the strongest predictor of mental health, as compared to other sources of social support (e.g., friends and family), thus supporting H1. This finding of a stronger association between leader versus co-worker and non-work-related sources of support adds specific information to and supplements previous research and theoretical reasoning. For example, LMX theory (Graen & Uhl-Bien, 1995; Gottfredson & Aquinis, 2017) claims that supportive behavior from leaders is of particular importance to employees' strain reactions.

Also Ganster and colleagues' (1986) study of 326 employees in a contracting firm showed that sources of support from the workplace, especially from the leader, are crucial in affecting stressors and strain, as compared to support resources that are not directly work related. However, the present finding runs contrary to the study of 211 traffic enforcement agents, who showed that family support was more closely associated with health-related outcomes such as burnout than with satisfaction and productivity, whilst immediate supervisor support was related to satisfaction and productivity but not burnout (Baruch-Felman, Brondolo, Ben-Dayan & Schwartz, 2002).

One reason for the different findings regarding the extent of impact from different sources of social support on health may be due to the dissimilar organizational conditions under study. According to LaRocco, House and French (1980), occupational task structure and environment may play a role in determining which role of support is the most salient. For instance, in occupations where employees are performing structured and repetitive tasks, productivity may be a more salient concern for leaders which may also have more training in addressing work-related outcomes versus stress-related responses (Baruch-Feldman et al., 2002).

Psychologists, on the other hand, may work with more human-related issues, and Norwegian psychologist-leaders, in addition to authority and autonomy, may have the necessary human- or stress-related skill to provide support for individuals' health-related reactions, i.e., understanding the signs and causes of stress and what can be done to help, which is central to most psychologists in Norway. According to Rønnestad and Skovholt (2003), disappointments with self and with inadequate client progress can fuel a sense of inadequacy. Hence, many counsellors will look for workplace mentors who will offer guidance and support. In the Rønnestad and Skovholt study, people most often mentioned were clients, professional elders (i.e., supervisors, personal therapists, professors, mentors), professional peers, friends, family members, and, later in one's career, younger colleagues.

The results of the present study indicate that social support from leaders may be of particular relevance for the mental health of psychologists. The main effect of leader support can be explained through the different functions of support itself. According to the leadership literature, social support from leaders may promote the experience of positive emotions (Glasø, Notelaers & Skogstad, 2011) and fulfills social needs, e.g., the sense of belonging and feelings of recognition (Hetland, Hetland, Andreassen, Pallesen & Notelaers, 2011). Alternatively, the present findings may also be explained by the "lack" of leader support. According to Carayon (1995), lack of social support from leaders may act as a chronic job stressor in itself. Research on loneliness (Cacioppo, 2002) provides ample evidence of the anguish, longing, and despair experienced by individuals who either lack or have lost important relationships.

Yet, the findings of the present study show that leader support not only directly influences mental health, but also acts as a buffer in the relationship between perceived stress and mental health. This is in line with H2, suggesting that social support from leaders may help counsellors cope with their stress experience and accordingly prevent it from impacting on health. Also Dormann and Zapf (1999) found a buffering effect on depression of social support from leaders in a three-wave study among citizens in Germany, using a time lag of 8 months. A possible account for this may be explained by the job-demand control-social support model (Karasek & Theorell, 1990), suggesting that job social support may facilitate successful coping with high-strain jobs (i.e., jobs with high demands, low control), as well as preventing or buffering the potentially harmful effects of these kinds of jobs. Following this notion, it is likely that counsellors, who have more access to leader support, may deal with work strain more effectively than those who experience less social support from leaders.

Further, while H2 proposes that leader support intervenes after stress perception by reducing the severity of the stress response, the results of the present study also support an indirect effect of social support, in that leader support directly influences perceived stress and subsequently the probability of ill-health. This means that social support may have a stress-preventive effect. This finding, supporting H3, is in line with Thomas and Lankau (2009), who found that supporting leader behavior (measured in terms of LMX) serve as resources that minimize emotional exhaustion through decreased role stress. Theoretically this may be explained by the job demand-resources model (Bakker, Demerouti, DeBoer, & Schaufeli 2003), suggesting that leader support may alleviate the influence of perceived stress on health, because leaders' appreciation and support may take away the burden of profound demands. For example, by responding positively to followers' needs for support, autonomy, role clarity, and reduced ambiguity, leaders may substantially reduce work stress (Humphrey, Nahrgang & Morgeson, 2007). On the other hand, by ignoring the above issues or other factors, such as role overload or subordinates' needs for involvement, leaders may contribute significantly to followers' perceptions of such stressors (Bass, 1990; Nelson, Basu & Purdie, 1998). In sum, the results support the notion that leaders' behaviour is important with regard to subordinates' health, and show that there are multiple pathways through which leader support can influence mental health among counsellors.

Methodological Issues

It is important to note that the findings are captured from a cross-sectional survey study. This may indicate single source challenges or problems since independent variables and the dependent variable are mapped at the same point in time. Common method variance refers to a possible response bias in survey research, and may have enhanced the overall strength of correlations (see Podsakoff, MacKenzie, Lee & Podsakoff, 2003). Since data are cross-sectional, causal inference among the variables cannot be made. Longitudinal studies may help clarify the causality. Moreover, we have no knowledge of how many or which of the respondents are working together as colleagues in the same organization. Thus, multi-level analysis is not an option here.

Data were collected by the assistance of the Norwegian Psychological Association (NPF), which means that all of respondents are member of that specific union. It could be the case that counsellors standing on the outside of the union may be different from those being represented by the union, for instance in terms of work experience or work sector that constitute their daily work arena. The study indicated a low variance and a low level in perceived stress and mental health problems among Norwegian counsellors. It could be that the level of stress or mental health problems may be higher among those being on the outside of the NPF, as they receive less professional help from their organized colleagues. However, the opposite could also be the case, were the group of non-organized counsellors may feel that they have a work day so free of substantial problems that they have no need of a membership in a union.

The present study is based on a large sample of counsellors, it has a relatively high participation rate, obtaining a response rate of 65 percent. It should be mentioned that the average response rate for studies that utilize data collected from individuals has been estimated to 53 percent, according to a meta study that captured the essence of 490 studies and 400 000 respondents (Baruch & Holtom, 2008).

Implications and Suggestion for Future Research

The present study has several practical implications. Firstly, as the results lend support to the notion that social support from leaders may have a direct and unique influence on subordinates' health as compared to other sources of social support, leaders should pay attention to their supporting role with regard to subordinates' mental health. Further, the findings that leader support influences subordinates' mental health in different ways highlights the importance of considering multiple perspectives in understanding the leaders' behavior and subordinates' health. Accordingly, different intervention strategies may be used to prevent work-related health problems among counsellors. For example, the moderating role of leader support suggests that leaders are in a position to influence or reduce stress-related reactions of more unchangeable inherent job characteristics (e.g., dealing with difficult client behavior).

Further, the indirect influence of leader support on health through stress perception implies that social support not only intervenes after the perception of stress and exerts its effect by reducing the severity of the stress responses, but also may reduce stress perception. Yet it should be noted that the moderator analysis shows that perceived stress also has a major effect on mental health, indicating that counsellors experience stress independent of social support variables. This implies that stress management strategies should focus on both the reduction of harmful work characteristics, such as the other demands of therapeutic work, as well as such positive factors as leader support.

The present study also has implications with regard to future research. Firstly, investigating of leader support with regard to other outcomes than mental health would be fruitful in order to further understand the counsellors' work situation. Further, we encourage more systematic research into the question of whether some types of social support (e.g., instrumental, informational, and emotional support) are more or less important for specific health outcomes, as well as whether different sources of support (e.g., work related, non-work-related) may have different effects on health outcomes. Finally, longitudinal studies addressing leader support and both potential positive and negative health-related outcomes are clearly warranted.

Conclusion

The present study shows that leader support predicts counsellors' mental health more than peer support, family support and friend support, and that leader support moderates the effect of stress on mental health. As such, this paper contributes to an increased understanding of counsellors' need of social support, especially from their immediate superior. Learning about counsellors' need of social support is important in order to know how to keep and enhance their well-being and mental health, which again may ensure a high standard of quality when they execute their profession. Achieving a comprehensive understanding of counsellors' need of social support may also help us prohibit any negative factors related to their professional conduct, such as incompetence, impairment and burnout.

Acknowledgments

We thank S. T. Engebråten, and A. M. Husø for their valuable contribution in collection of the data employed in the present study.

References

Ackerley, G. D., Burnell, J., Holder, D. C., & Kardek, L. A. (1988). Burnout among licenced psychologists. *Professional Psychology: Research and Practice, 19*, 624-631.

Amundsen, S. & Martinsen, Ø.L. (2014): Empowering leadership: Construct clarification, conceptualization, and validation of a new scale. *Leadership Quarterly, 25*, 487–511.

Baker, E. K. (2003). Caring for ourselves: A therapist's guide to personal and professional well-being, (pp. 37-58). Washington, DC, US: *American Psychological Association*, ix, 173 pp.

Bakker, A. B., Demerouti, E., De Boer, E., & Schaufeli, W. B. (2003). Job demands and job resources as predictors of absence duration and frequency. *Journal of Vocational Behavior, 62*, 341-56.

Barling, J., Bluen, S. D., & Fain, R. (1987). Psychological functioning following an acute disaster. *Journal of Applied Psychology, 72*, 683–690.

Baron, M. R., & Kenny, D. A. (1986). The Moderator-Mediator Variable Distinction in Social Psychological Research: Conceptual, Strategic and Statistical Considerations. *Journal of Personality and Social Psychology, 51*(6), 1173-1182.

Baruch, Y., & Holtom, B. C. (2008). Survey response rate levels and trends in organizational research. *Human Relations, 61*(8), 1139-1160.

Baruch-Felman, C., Brondolo, E., Ben-Dayan, D., & Schwartz, J. (2002). Sources of social support and burnout, job satisfaction, and productivity. *Journal of Occupational Health Psychology, 7*, 84–93.

Bearse, J. L., McMinn, M. R., Seegobin, W., & Free, K. (2013). Barriers to psychologists seeking mental health care. Professional Psychology: Research and Practice, 44, 150–157.

Beehr, T. A. (1985). The role of social support in coping with organizational stress. In T.A. Beehr and R.S. Bhagat (Eds.), *Human stress and cognition in organizations: An integrated perspective.* New York: John Wiley & Sons.

Beehr, T. (1995). *Psychological stress in the workplace.* London: Routledge.

Cacioppo, J. T., Hawkley, L. C., Crawford, L. E., Ernst, J. M., Burleson, M. H., Kowalewski, R. B., Malarkey, W. B., Van Cauter, E., & Berntson, G. G. (2002). Loneliness and health: Potential mechanisms. *Psychosomatic Medicine, 64*, 407-417.

Carayon, P. (1995). Chronic effect of job control, supervisor social support, and work pressure on office worker stress. In S. L. Sauter & L. R. Murphy (Eds.), *Organizational risk factors for job stress* (pp. 357-370). Washington, DC: American Psychological Association.

Cartwright, S. (2010). Job Demands, Resources and Psychological and Physical Well-being: Critical Factors Which May Make Some Jobs More Stressful Than Others. In R. J. Burke & C. L. Cooper (Eds.), *Risky Business: Psychological and behavioural aspects of risk in organizations* (pp. 263-286). England: Gower Publishing Limited.

Collins, A.M., Hislop, D., & Cartwright, S. (2016). Social support in the workplace between teleworkers, office-based colleagues, and supervisors. *New Technology, Work and Employment. 31* (2), 161-175.

Deutsch, C. J. (1984). Self-reported sources of stress among psychotherapists. *Professional Psychology: Research and Practice, 15*, 833-845.

Dorman, C. & Zapf, D. (1999). Social support, social stressors at work, and depressive symptoms: Testing for main and moderating effects with structural equations in a three-wave longitudinal study. *Journal of Applied Psychology, 84(6),* 874-884.

Farber, B. A. (1990). Burnout in psychotherapists: incidence, types, and trends. *Psychotherapy in Private Practice, 8*, 35-44.

Frese, M. (1999). Social support as a moderator of the relationship between work stressors and psychological dysfunctioning: A longitudinal study with objective measures. *Journal of Occupational Health Psychology, 4,* 179–192.

Ganster, D. C., Fusilier, M. R., & Mayes, B. T. (1986). Role of social support in the experience of stress at work. *Journal of Applied Psychology, 71,* 102-110.

Gardner, D., & O'Driscoll, M. (2007). Professional wellbeing. In I. M. Evans, J. J. Rucklidge & M. O' Driscoll (Eds.), *Professional Practice of Psychology in Aotearoa New Zealand* (pp. 245-258).Wellington, New Zealand: The New Zealand Psychological Society Inc.

Glasø, L., Bele, E., Nielsen, B. M., & Einarsen, S. (2011). Bus drivers' exposure to bullying at work: An occupation-specific approach. *Scandinavian Journal of Psychology, 52,* 484-493.

Glasø, L., Notelaers, G. & Skogstad, A. (2011). The importance of followers' emotions in effective leadership. *Scandinavian Journal of Organizational Psychology, 3*(2), 17-31

Glasø, L., Skogstad, A., Notelaers, G., & Einarsen, S. (2017). Leadership, affect and outcomes: Symmetrical and asymmetrical relationships, *Leadership & Organizational Development Journal. Doi* 10.1108/LODJ-08-2016-0194.

Goldberg, D. (1978). *Manual of the General Health Questionnaire*, Windsor: NFER-Nelson.

Goldberg, D., & Williams, P. (1988). *A user's guide to the general health questionnaire*. London: Nfer-Nelson.

Gottfredson, R. & Aguinis, H. (2017): Leadership behaviors and follower performance: Deductive and inductive examination of theoretical rationales and underlying mechanisms. *Journal of Organizational Behavior*, *38*, 558–591.

Graen, G. B., & Uhl-Bien, M. (1995). Relationship-based approach to leadership: Development of leader-member exchange (LMX) theory of leadership over 25 years: Applying a multi-level multi-domain perspective. *The Leadership Quarterly, 6*(2), 219-247.

Graham, L. N., & Witteloostuijn, A. V. (2010). Leader–member exchange communication frequency and burnout. *Discussion Paper Series #10–08*, Utrecht School of Economics, Tjalling C. Koopmans Research Institute.

Greenglass, E. R., Fiksenbaum, L., & Burke, R. J. (1994). The relationship between social support and burnout over time in teachers. *Journal of Social Behavior and Personality, 9*, 219–230.

Guy, J. D., Poelstra, P. L., & Stark, M. J. (1989). Personal distress and therapeutic effectiveness: national survey of psychologists practicing psychotherapy. *Professional Psychology: Research and Practice, 20*, 48-50.

Hannigan, B., Edwards, D., & Bernard, P. (2004). Stress and stress management in clinical psychology: Findings from a systematic review. *Journal of Mental Health, 13*, 235–245.

Harris, K. J., & Kacmar, K. M. (2005). Easing the strain: The buffer role of supervisors in the perceptions of politics–strain relationship. *Journal of Occupational and Organizational Psychology, 78*, 337–354.

Harris, K. J., & Kacmar, K. M. (2006). Too Much of a Good Thing: The Curvilinear Effect of Leader–Member Exchange on Stress. *The Journal of Social Psychology, 146*, 65-84.

Hetland, H., Hetland, J., Andreassen, C. S., Pallesen, S., & Notelaers, G. (2011). Leadership and fulfillment of the three basic psychological needs at work. *Career Development International, 16*(5), 507-523.

House, J. S. (1981). *Work stress and social support*. Reading, MA: Addison-Wesley.

Huang, X., Chan, S. C. H., Lam, W., & Nan, X. (2010). The joint effect of leader–member exchange and emotional intelligence on burnout and work performance in call centers in China. *International Journal of Human Resource Management, 21*, 1124-1144.

Humphrey, S. E., Nahrgang, J. D., & Morgeson, F. P. (2007). Integrating motivational, social and contextual work design features: A meta-analytic summary and theoretical extension of the work design literature. *Journal of Applied Psychology, 92(5), 1332 1356. doi:10.1037/0021-9010.92.5.1332.*

Karasek, R., & Theorell, T. (1990). *Healthy work: stress, productivity, and the reconstruction of working life*. New York: Basic Books.

Kaufmann, G. M., & Beehr, T. A. (1986). Interactions between job stressors and social support: Some counterintuitive results. *Journal of Applied Psychology, 71*, 522-526.

Kelloway, E. K., Sivanathan, N., Francis, L., & Barling, J. (2005). Poor leadership. In J. Barling, E. K. Kelloway & M. R. Frone (Eds.), *Handbook of work stress*. Thousand Oaks, CA: Sage.

Kickul, J., & Posig, M. (2001). Supervisory Emotional Support and Burnout: An Explanation of Reverse Buffering Effects. *Journal of Management Issues 13*(3), 328-344.

Kozlowski, S. W. J., & Doherty, M. L. (1989). Integration of Climate and Leadership: examination of a neglected issue. *Journal of Applied Psychology, 74*, 546-553.

LaRocco, J. M., House, J. S., & French, J. R. P. (1980). Social support, organizational stress and health. *Journal of Health and Social Behaviour, 21*, 202 -218.

Lazarus, R. S., & Folkman, S. (1984). *Stress, Appraisal and Coping.* New York: Springer.

Leavy, R. L. (1983). Social support and psychological disorder: A review. *Journal of Community Psychology, 11*, 3–21.

Lee, K.-E. (2011). Moderating effects of leader-member exchange (LMX) on job burnout in dietitians and chefs of institutional foodservice. *Nutrition Research Practice, 5*(1), 80–87.

Mahoney, M. J. (1997). Psychotherapists' personal problems and selfcare patterns. *Professional Psychology: Research and Practice, 28,* 14-16.

Ng, T. W. H. (2017). Transformational leadership and performance outcomes: Analyses of multiple mediation pathways. *The Leadership Quarterly, 28,* 385-417. DOI: 10.1016/j.leaqua.2016.11.008.

Nissen-Lie, H.A., Monsen, J. T., Ulleberg., P., & Rønnestad, M. H. (2013). Psychotherapists' self-reports of their interpersonal functioning and difficulties in practice as predictors of patient outcome. *Psychotherapy Research, 23*(1), 86-104.

Penninkilampi-Kerola, V., Miettunen, J., & Ebeling, H. (2006). A comparative assessment of the factor structures and psychometric properties of the GHQ-12 and the GHQ-20 based on data from a Finnish population-based sample. *Scandinavian Journal of Psychology, 47*(5), 431-440. doi:10.1111/j.1467-9450.2006.00551.x

Orlinsky, D.E., & Rønnestad, M. H. (2005). *How Psychotherapists Develop: A Study of Therapeutc Work and Professional Growth.* Washington, DC: American Psychological Association.

Orlinsky, D. E. & Rønnestad, Michael Helge (2013). Positive and negative cycles of practitioner development: Evidence, concepts and implications from a collaborative quantitative study of psychotherapists, In *The developing practitioner: Growth and stagnation of therapists and counselors* (Chapter 14, pp 265 – 290). Routledge. ISBN 978-0-415-88459-4.

O'disroll, M. P. & Beehr, T. (1994). Supervisor behaviors, role stressors and uncertainty as predictors of personal outcomes for subordinates. *Journal of Organizational Behavior, 15*, 141-55.

Podsakoff, P. M., MacKenzie, S. B., Lee, J. Y., & Podsakoff, N. (2003). Common method biases in behavioural research: A critical review of the literature and recommended remedies. *Journal of Applied Psychology, 88*, 879-903.

Rupert, P. A., & Morgan, D. J., (2005). Work setting and burnout among professional psychologists. *Professional Psychology: Research and Practice, 36*, 544–550.

Rupert, P. A., Stevanovic, P., & Hunley, H. A. (2009). Work–family conflict and burnout among professional psychologists. *Professional Psychology: Research and Practice, 40*, 54–61.

Rønnestad. M. H., & Skovholt, T.M. (2013). The Journey of the Counselor and Therapist: Research Findings and Perspectives on Professional Development. *Journal of Career Development, 30*(1), 5-44.

Simmons, B. L., & Nelson, D. L. (2001). Eustress at work: The relationship between hope and health in hospital nurses. *Health Care Management Review, 26*(4), 7-18.

Skakon, J., Nielsen, K., Borg, V., & Guzman, J. (2010). Are leaders' well-being, behaviours and style associated with the affective well-being of their employees? A systematic review of three decades of research. *Work and Stress, 24,* 107–139.

Smith, P. L., & Moss, S. B. (2009). Psychologist impairment: What is it, how can it be prevented, and what can be done to address it? *Clinical Psychology: Science and Practice, 16*(1), 1-15.

Skogstad, A., Hetland, J., Glasø, L., & Einarsen, S. (2014). Is avoidant leadership a root cause of subordinate stress? Longitudinal relationships between laissez-faire leadership and role ambiguity, *Work and Stress, 4,* 323-341.

Stevanovic, P., & Rupert, P. A. (2004). Career-sustaining behaviors, satisfactions and stresses of professional psychologists. *Psychotherapy: Theory Research and Practice, 41*(3), 301-309.

Thanacoody, P.R., Bartram, T., & Casimir, G. (2009). The effects of burnout and supervisory social support on the relationship between work-family conflict and intention to leave: A study of Australian cancer workers. *Journal of Health Organization and Management, 23*(1), 53-69.

Tepper, B. J. (2000). Consequences of Abusive Supervision. *Academy of Management Journal, 43,* 178-190.

Thériault, A., & Gazzola, N. (2005). Feelings of inadequacy, insecurity, and incompetence among experienced therapists. *Counselling and Psychotherapy Research*, **5**, 11-18.

Thomas, C. H., & Lankau, M. J. (2009). Preventing burnout: the effects of LMX and mentoring on socialization, role stress, and burnout. *Human Resource Management, 48,* 417–432.

van Daalen, G., Sanders, K., & Willemsen, T. M. (2005). Sources of social support as predictors of health, psychological well-being and life satisfaction among Dutch male and female dual-earners. *Women and Health, 41*, 43–62.

Van der Doef, M., & Maes, S. (1999). The job demand-control (-support) model and psychological well-being: A review of 20 years of empirical research. *Work and Stress, 13,* 87–114.

Viswesvaran, C., Sanches, J. I., & Fisher, J. (1999). The role of social support in the process of work stress: A Meta-Analysis. *Journal of Vocational Behavior, 54,* 314-334.

Wolfgang A. P. (1988). The health professions stress inventory. *Psychological Reports, 62,* 220–222.

Sectoral State Traditions – A Tool to Study Convergence of National Ideas in Policymaking

Marit Sjøvaag

BI, Norwegian Business School, Norway

ABSTRACT

The sustainability of distinctive national policymaking traditions has been questioned in writings on ideas and their role in the policymaking process. This article proposes an operationalisation of national policymaking traditions that enables cross-national longitudinal comparison: sectoral state traditions, thus contributing to the ongoing debate about the role of ideas in policymaking. Sectoral state traditions are defined as a set of ideas about political authority and legitimate state action in the relevant sector, expressed and identified through public political discourse, which is a major vehicle to maintain and develop traditions in policymaking.

The concept is useful in analysing cross-national convergence of ideas as shown by an investigation of institutional reforms in the telephone policy area in the period 1876-1997.

Thus, the key findings in this article suggest that policy convergence does not equate convergence of ideas.

Key Words: sectoral state traditions, ideas in policymaking, convergence, political discourse

Introduction: The importance of ideas

Ideas matter in politics. Exactly how they exert influence, induce change or maintain stability is less clear. One hurdle in the scholarly debate on ideas in politics regards operationalisation of ideas; which 'set of beliefs' to include as relevant, and which ones to disregard.

This article comprises five parts. First, it discusses some of the challenges of the literature on ideas and state traditions. Second, it argues the case for investigating change in sectoral state traditions. Third, it discusses the role of political discourse in maintaining and identifying sectoral state traditions. Fourth, it defines and details the concepts of 'sectoral state traditions'. Finally, the article illustrates the usefulness of this concept based on a longitudinal study of sectoral state traditions in the telephone sector in France and Germany.

Political science analyses are increasingly paying attention to ideas, as interests and institutions alone are inadequate as full explanation of policy development (Majone 1992; Elster 1989; Schmidt 2000; Béland 2009; Kersbergen and Vis 2014). Rationalist and institutionalist models, which mostly see policies as a result of a process in which rational actors strive for outcomes that match their own preferences as closely as possible, generally do not seek to analyse the role of ideas (Marsden and Reardon 2017). However, "even if we accept the rationality premise, actions taken by human beings depend on the substantive quality of available ideas, since such ideas help to clarify principles and conceptions of causal relationships, and to coordinate individual behavior" (Goldstein and Keohane 1993: 5).

Moreover, ideas about what is politically legitimate in a particular national and sectoral setting "affect groups' perceptions of their interest and foster in them a disposition to explain their positions in abstract terms, to fit their particular concerns into a larger framework" (Dyson 1980: 3). Ideas at this level thus influence the frames within which politics are to be conducted, i.e. rules for 'what just is and isn't done', what factors should be included in relevant futures, and they help to identify who are members of a political community (Kvistad 1999; Andersen and Rasmussen 2014). In the political process, commitment to common ideas and purposes is useful because it "creates 'will', and widespread agreement produces legitimacy" (Orren 1988: 27).

According to Goldstein and Keohane (1993) ideas (defined as 'beliefs held by individuals') principally have three functions in policymaking: they serve as roadmaps; they assist in consolidating outcomes in the absence of a unique equilibrium; and because they (sometimes but not always) become institutionalised, they sustain the influence of actors' interests even in cases where the actors themselves or their interests have changed.

However, their focus on the *effect* of ideas rather than the ideas themselves, i.e. their assertion that ideas influence policymaking when they fall into one of the categories cited above, complicates (indeed, renders questionable) the task of identifying ideas other than strictly programmatic ones. Ideas affect policy outcome, but the role of these ideas is confused because their impact may simply reflect the interests of actors. It therefore seems difficult if not impossible to separate cases where ideas exert their own independent influence from cases where a traditional interest analysis would provide adequate analysis. Moreover, in addition to the difficulty in showing any causal relationship between ideas and policy outcomes, their approach suffers from great difficulties in defining which 'beliefs held by individuals', of which there are many, are relevant to policymaking.

Favell (2001) envisages ideas as systems of meaning. For political debate to be meaningful, actors need to agree on certain basic assumptions. Favell's 'official political theory' is a consistent argument about a political issue that actors adhere to. Such a theory includes guidance on how to interpret basic facts (epistemological claims); causal beliefs about means and ends (explanatory claims); and core values specifying the ideal end-goal (normative claims). An 'official political theory', however, is not a theory in a strict scientific sense, but rather a 'workable compromise' resulting from the political process. It thus shares important similarities with Hall's (1993) policy paradigm, "a framework of ideas and standards that specifies not only the goal of policy and the kind of instruments that can be used to attain them, but also the very nature of the problems they are meant to be addressing" (Hall 1993: 279). Like Hall's paradigms Favell's 'official political theories' can change, under similar conditions of long-term sub-optimality or political crisis. Favell's definition of an 'official political theory' is useful because it provides an analytical tool that operates on a 'medium level' of ideas: his 'official theory' is wider than simple programmatic statements, but because of its quality of 'workable compromise' remains less extensive and less abstract than a fully-fledged political theory.

The 'advocacy coalition framework' (Sabatier and Jenkins-Smith 1993; Jenkins-Smith and

Sabatier 1994; Sabatier and Schlager 2000) distinguishes between 'core' and 'secondary' beliefs, where the core beliefs comprise elements such as scope for government intervention in the economy, and for degree of centralisation in government functions. Core beliefs, similar to 'sectoral state traditions', are hypothesised to be relatively stable over a decade or more, and form the basis around which policy coalitions are formed. The basic assumption about long-term stability of core beliefs is not tested in the advocacy coalition framework, mostly because the focus of the advocacy coalition framework is on explaining policy output and policy change.

Thus, the introduction of 'ideas' into political sciences analyses has not always resulted in increased clarity regarding the ideas themselves or their role in policymaking. There are two main reasons for this. A major problem with the body of political science literature concerned with 'ideas' is that there is no general agreement as to the *content* of relevant ideas. A wide range of ideas has been studied, from relatively narrow 'programmatic ideas', or policy programmes (Jacobsen 1997; Notermans 1998; Woods 1995; Goldstein 1989; Blyth 2001), to broad ideas about the nature of the state and political theories. Studies on narrow, programmatic ideas suffer from an inherent difficulty in distinguishing between the role of the ideas themselves, and the power of their advocates, thus questioning the potential value added to traditional interest based models. The broader concepts of state traditions and political theory, however, are difficult to operationalise in a specific policy setting, and it remains unclear how such broad ideas could be seen to influence either the policy process or the outcome.

The second major difficulty for the literature on ideas is related to how ideas have been studied. Much literature on ideas has been criticised for failing to show what role ideas have in the policy process (Kohler-Koch 2002), which is not surprising, given the imprecise nature of much of the 'ideas' under investigation. However, most analyses of ideas and their effect on policymaking use *policies* as indicator of whether ideas have influence the policy process, instead of studying the arena where ideas are likely to be used more determinedly by policymakers, i.e. in political discourse.

Recent studies of ideas thus often suffer from a difficulty in identifying and analysing the ideas themselves rather than their probable effect on the policymaking process and on policies. This contribution suggests using public political discourse rather than policies as an indicator of sectoral state traditions.

The 'State Traditions' Concept

Studies on 'state traditions' narrow the range of ideas under investigation, from broad definitions such as 'beliefs held by individuals' to conceptions about the role and authority of state in society. The term 'state tradition' has been used by scholars to emphasise aspects of political life that are directly related to the existence of cognition of a 'state', and as such finds its place in the wider literature on the role of ideas in policymaking. 'State tradition', as opposed to 'national traditions', has an immediate interpretation of 'something belonging to or emanating from the state apparatus', and most analyses involving state traditions emphasise the cognitive aspect.

Dyson's (1980) seminal work contrasts 'state societies' (typically found in Continental Europe) with 'stateless societies' (Britain and the US being his foremost examples) and identifies a set of characteristics for 'state societies':

- 'State societies' have a conception of 'public power';
- They deny that the public interest is only the sum of private interests, and so exemplify non-economic, non-utilitarian attitudes to political relations;
- They stress the distinctiveness of state and society, whether in terms of the special function of the state or in terms of the peculiar character of its authority;
- They have a concern with institutions, reflecting legalism and codification, as well as de-personalisation of the public power;
- They display a moralistic view of politics which involves strongly collectivist and regulatory attitudes (Dyson 1980: 51-52).

The 'state' thus functions as a *generalising*, *integrating*, and *legitimating* concept. It is *generalising* because it combines political society with ideas of collectivity and the general good, *integrating* because it integrates an array of institutions either through centralism (as in France) or through co-ordination of autonomous units loyal to the federation (as in Germany). Its *legitimating* aspects imply that institutions and individuals are seen as elements in a political community whose coherence and unity are established by the explicit articulation, identification, and ordering of certain principles and norms (Dyson 1980: 208-214).

Dyson's study (1980) also outlines a conceptual model to classify states where the perceived legitimate political action is closely connected to the nature of authority in a society. For continental European countries, the 'state' is seen as the "institution of political rule" (Dyson 1980: vii), so that an increased understanding of the nature of the 'state' can be said to increase the understanding of the political processes. The state concept has some common elements across countries: it "identifies the leading values of the political community with reference to which authority is to be exercised; emphasizes the distinctive character and unity of the 'public power' compared with civil society; focuses on the need for depersonalisation of the exercise of that power; finds its embodiment in one or more institutions and one or more public purposes which thereby acquire a special ethos and prestige and an association with the public interest or general welfare; and produces a social-cultural awareness of (and sometimes dissociation from) the unique and superior nature of the state itself" (Dyson 1980: 206). The values, institutionalisation of the depersonalisation of power, and public purposes themselves, however, vary between states, and can also vary within states over time.

Other authors have applied the term 'state traditions' in their analyses. Grimm (1991) gives an overview of the major political and intellectual events from the sixteenth century onwards as they relate to central characteristics of the state in continental Europe, in which he focuses on the intellectual reasoning and ideas behind state authority and sovereignty in relation to society. Rohe (1993) analyses the German state traditions as political culture, emphasising the existence of three different sub-cultures (dominant, Catholic and Socialist), the relative weakness of '*Gesellschaftskultur*' ('society culture', or the allegiance to the macro-level in society) compared to '*Gemeinschaftskultur*' ('community culture', or allegiance to smaller, club-like entities) and maintains that the problem of mediating between the political system and civil society remains in German political culture. Laborde (2000) reassesses the importance of the concept of state in British and French political thought. Her study primarily argues that the 'statelessness' of Britain is greatly overstated, but it also contributes to the refinement of the picture of the existence of a strong state concept in France.

State traditions therefore, as presented in literature, contribute to the study of ideas a precision of the ideas under investigation. *State traditions are thus a specific set of ideas relating to the normative distribution of power and authority in society, and to the institutionalisation of such norms*. State traditions are seen to contribute to individual policymakers' perception of politics, to socialising policymakers and to providing shared norms for a policy community. State traditions confine the range of policy options because of the limits they set on cognitive processes. Policies that are perceived as contradicting the state tradition will be seen as lacking in legitimacy and thus be difficult, or even impossible, to implement, if indeed they are even considered. State traditions are expressed as values in political discourse. However, a state tradition is not necessarily unchangeable and static; it can be manipulated and changed from within, as well as altered in response to exogenous forces.

The major difficulty with analysing state traditions is their level of generality, which complicates the operationality of the concept. Ideas on the role of the state and on the ideal distribution of authority and power in society are so vast and so complex that analysis must remain general. This article proposes to meet this problem by applying the general state traditions model to a sector-specific setting. The sectoral state tradition concept used here is therefore a subset of state traditions that is relevant to a particular sector. It embodies a notion of authority and of who should be the relevant actors in the policy process and what should be their relevant power. It also encompasses public ethos of the state and of sectoral policies, as well as criteria for legitimate decision-making procedures and discourse.

Change in Ideas and State Traditions

State traditions are not static. They 'idea of the state' is by its very nature open-textured (Dyson 1980: 2), and its meaning depends on the context in which it is used. Although the chronological change in the idea of the state is not the major part of Dyson's work (his main focus being the link between the idea of the state and society), he nevertheless concludes that "a sense of direction [of the development of the idea of the 'state'] is only likely to be achieved if philosophy is prepared to marry conceptual analysis to a more comprehensive, historical understanding of social and political experience" (Dyson 1980: 287). Despite this call for further research, he sketches a development where the Western European 'state' can be said to experience (in the late 1970s) a sense of 'crisis'. He illustrates this tendency with growing international interdependence, both economically and politically, partly through the increased sense of the failure of the traditional state to tackle contemporary problems.

Other approaches to change include Hall's (1993) work on policy paradigms and social learning. If policy paradigms (defined as a framework of ideas and standards that specify policy goals, the appropriate instruments, and the nature of the problem) are to change, the change is likely to be associated with a process in which the overarching terms of policy discourse radically change. A movement from one paradigm to another is also likely to be preceded by significant shifts in the locus of authority over policy. Since ideas form a major part of a policy paradigm, a paradigm change can be seen to indicate a change in ideas, and potential paradigm changes are thus identified by radical changes in the political discourse, by politicisation of the issue, and by a change in locus of authority (Hall 1993: 279).

Hall's model is of interest here because it uses discourse as the main indicator of a policy paradigm, and because the ideas he includes in his 'third-order change' resemble those in the sectoral state tradition. It does however remain unclear from his model whether a paradigm shift (and thus change in ideas) is possible without major change among the policymaker individuals, and without a change in the governing political parties. If ideas (paradigms, sectoral state tradition) cannot change while the actors remain constant, it might be impossible to draw conclusions about the independent power of ideas.

'Ideas' are also referred to, albeit less stringently, in a host of studies on policy convergence (Dolowitz and March 2000; Bennett 1991; Peters 1997; Eatwell 1997; Levy 1997). Although the 'ideas' mentioned in these works mostly are not the type of ideas included in a sectoral state tradition, there seems to be a 'common (mis)belief' that ways of thinking about the nature of a problem (i.e. ideas) become increasingly similar as policy converges across countries. Ikenberry (1990), in his study of the spread of privatisation policies, argues that change in policies can indicate either a change in the state's goals, or a change in what instruments it sees as appropriate to reach its goal. The 'wave' of privatisation in the 1990s was evidence that governments from across the world increasingly valued efficiency as one goal of public policies, although they previously had (supposedly) different ideas about the value of efficiency. This emphasis on efficiency across the world can thus be interpreted as a convergence of (certain) ideas.

The argument that convergent policies indicate convergent ideas becomes even more pronounced in writing on 'globalisation'. "Globalization is not undermining the state system, but it is producing increasingly strong pressures for states to be of a certain sort – open, democratic, flexible, and respectful of the rule of law" (Ikenberry 1997: 2). Economic imperatives linked to an open world economy (e.g., similar socio-economic environments, common pressures through transnational networks of interest groups or politicians) give governments less room for choice, and their policies become more similar (Eatwell 1997; True and Mintrom 2001; Cerny 2000; Wolman 1992; Dolowitz and March 2000; Mahnig and Wimmer 2016). Globalisation, promoting change through economic and industrial interdependence, is thus seen to foster not only similar solutions across countries, but indeed similar policy goals, such as economic efficiency and international competitiveness.

Thus, although only rarely explicit, studies on policy convergence have shown a tendency to assume that convergent policies indicate convergent ideas, not only about policy measures, but also about goals for state activity.

Discourse as Indicator of Sectoral State Traditions

Political discourse is an important vehicle for the communication, maintenance, and development of state traditions. As Dyson (1980: 1) comments, "[l]anguage is part of the social and political structure; it reveals the politics of a society". Language is an active tool in the political process. The way in which issues are approached, and what concepts are employed, helps to determine the ensuing politicking, the issues' chances of reaching the agenda of a particular institution, and the final outcome (Rochefort and Cobb 1994: 9). "Issue definition is central to studies of (…) politics (…) because different definitions generate different cleavages in society. Public debate and policymaking concerning important policy issues rarely consider all elements of an issue at once" (Baumgartner and Jones 1994: 50).

Discourse is therefore a good indicator of sectoral state traditions. Although political discourse should not be taken *prima facie* as expressing the 'true' beliefs and values of the speaker, or be seen to be solely produced (as a cynic might suggest) in order to manipulate the policy community or the general public into accepting prominence of certain interests, it nevertheless reveals the speaker's perception of the environment's requests for legitimate behaviour. Discourse is also increasingly used as a tool in policymaking analysis (Wilkerson, Smith and Stramp 2015; Winkel and Leipold 2016).

Using 'discourse' as an indicator of sectoral state traditions is, however, not limited to study the concepts used in public debate, which essentially (although not exclusively) focus on public ethos. The *form* of discourse is a good indicator of the relative power of policymakers. In her analysis of how discourse impacts on the political process Vivien Schmidt (2002; 2000) distinguishes between communicative and coordinative discourse. The former is prevalent in states where policymaking is predominantly centralised, determined among an inner group, and communicated to the public only when the decisions have been made. Conversely, the coordinative discourse is more common in countries where policymaking is more dispersed, and where larger parts of the population are involved in negotiating reform. Coordinative discourse is mainly aimed at knowledgeable co-deciders, and tends to be more technical than communicative discourse. Thus, a public discourse of either of these types indicates how policymakers perceive rules for legitimate decision-making. A communicative discourse indicates that policymakers are confident that policies, once agreed upon by the relevant actors (which, because of the communicative nature of the discourse, excludes the general public), are legitimate. A coordinative discourse, however, points to greater dispersion of power among the relevant actors, and (ideally) greater possibilities for the general public to participate.

Discourse is thus used to indicate the way in which policymakers frame the issues at hand, and to decipher (hidden) assumptions; what is taken for granted and what remains unquestioned by policymakers. To the extent that state traditions are explicitly known and expressed, policymakers can manipulate the framing of emerging issues and certain preferred solutions so they are adhering to the principles of the state tradition, thus increasing their perceived legitimacy in a policy community.

Analysing Sectoral State Traditions

The establishment of sectoral state traditions as analytical tool enables analysis of the persistence (or not) of ideas in national policymaking. Three aspects are of particular importance if the concept is to be of analytical use: First, the types of ideas present in a sectoral state tradition. Second, the original sectoral state tradition must be established to give a starting point for analysis of change or continuity. Third, a method for identifying change must be established.

Defining Sectoral State Traditions: Central Elements

A sectoral state tradition is a sub-set of state traditions relevant to a particular sector. The constitutive elements are chosen based on the theoretical works outlined earlier, in particular the elements identified as belonging to the (Continental European) state tradition by Dyson (1980). However, focus on a particular sector necessitates adjustments to Dyson's model. The 'notion of authority' and 'public ethos' remain central for sectoral state traditions. Moreover, the ideas about state as legitimating concept, and its implications for practical decision-making procedures and political discourse, are included in a sectoral state tradition. But all elements are interpreted with respect to the particular sectoral setting. This does not imply that the sectoral state traditions would contradict the general state traditions, but rather, that the level of detail regarding actors, institutions and legal framework is greater than if general state traditions were being studied. Furthermore, similar studies of different sectors might require further adjustments to capture essential sectoral characteristics. The list of elements presented here is therefore not necessarily exhaustive for all possible empirical cases, but should provide sufficiently general to be of use in cross-national, as well as cross-sectoral, comparisons.

A sectoral state tradition includes:

- A notion of authority and of who should be the relevant actors in the policy process, and an institutional framework delineating power structures between these;
- A public ethos of sectoral policies;
- Criteria for legitimate decision-making procedures and discourse.

Origin of a Sectoral State Tradition

Identifying a point at which a sectoral state tradition is consolidated is central to the question of whether such traditions remain stable over time. The search for state traditions, and for explanations of social organisation and state structures, can be drawn far back into the past.

However, practicalities necessitate limiting empirical research. The consolidation of a sectoral state tradition is expressed through the establishment of a language common to all interested parties, through which problems are perceived and solutions defined.

Determining Change in Sectoral State Traditions

Sectoral state traditions are ideas about political authority and legitimate state action in a specific sector. Identifying change can be difficult, because the identification in many cases must depend on subjective measurements (ideas, norms and values, are in most cases implicit rather than explicit). To minimise the risk of subjectivity in the process of determining change in sectoral state traditions certain parameters should be used as a 'checklist' to indicate stability or change. The parameters proposed are:

The Notion of Authority, Relevant Actors, and Their Relative Power

The formal institutional framework partly determines both relevant actors and their relative power. However, ideas about who should possess ultimate authority are not necessarily corresponding to the *de facto* power these actors have in practical policymaking. Because the essential elements of a sectoral state tradition are ideas about the ideal distribution of power, expressed in public political discourse, potential changes to such ideas must be evaluated by how policies are presented, rather than by how they were practically formed.

Public Ethos of Sectoral Policies

Common agreement on the identification of the sector's product is crucial to the maintenance of the state tradition. It establishes a common language for all interested parties and frames the relevant questions and issues in the sector based on shared values. If this consensus is questioned and a new consensus appears, the sectoral tradition can be said to have changed. It is, however, important to distinguish between the public ethos and its implications for policy instruments. A change in the latter (e.g., from direct state service provision to regulation of private service providers) does not necessarily imply change in public ethos, which depends on how the (new) policy instruments are legitimated in public political discourse.

Criteria for Legitimate Decision-Making and Discourse

Legitimate methods for policymaking involve formal and informal rules about who are consulted for new policy proposals and about the style of communication between these actors. The nature of the public discourse changes if central concepts identified in previous time periods are no longer in use, or are used significantly less, or if new concepts are given prominent place; if the set of participants in the public debate changes; or if new technological possibilities are couched in terms different from existing ones.

Is the Concept Useful? Lessons from Empirical Analysis

Determining whether sectoral state traditions converge require deep and broad analysis of policymaking discourse. The author has undertaken such analysis of the telephone policy regime in France and Germany for the period 1876-1997. Since sectoral state traditions are identified through public political discourse it is advantageous to use periods in which the policy area figures relatively prominently in public political debate. For this reason, the focus for the empirical investigation was on periods of institutional reform, more specifically: the consolidation phase up until c. 1900, when both France and Germany had achieved well-developed legislative regimes for telephone policy; the reforms of the 1920s, when similar exogenous pressures in the form of international calls for 'scientific management' were interpreted differently in the French and German case; the post-war regime; the corporatisation of the 1980s; and the privatisation of the 1990s.

For each of the five periods the sectoral state tradition was identified in both countries. Most of the elements of the sectoral state tradition remained relatively constant over time. The source of the ultimate authority remained *Parliament* in France (although it was challenged by the EU in the 1980s) and *legislation* in Germany. The French notion of *service public* retained its function as public ethos, despite its content being modified over time. The German ethos was slower to emerge, but revolved around principles of cost-efficiency and correction of economic dysfunctions. Criteria for legitimate decision-making (procedural correctness in France and bureaucratic correctness in Germany) remained stable throughout the period.

The major changes identified in the national sectoral state traditions were both on the French side, and both after the 1970s. The first change was that a new set of actors, namely those representing industry, became seen as relevant for sectoral policymaking in France. The second change was from communicative to coordinative discourse.

Can the identified changes in the French set of actors, criteria for legitimate decision-making and discourse, be interpreted as a convergence between the French and the German sectoral state traditions?

German policymaking traditionally involved business interests to a much larger extent than in France. German legal obligations to consult business interests and the involvement of the *Länder* ensured participation from a broader set of interests than the French centralist, elitist method. However, from the mid-1980s French policymaking incorporated more open consultation and more dialogue between government officials and business interest, similar to a German decision-making model. There were, however, important differences. Policymaking in France never reached the same degree of consensus-seeking as in Germany, and, more importantly, there were never any legal obligations on the public administration to consult the wider interests.

The use of open consultations in France was paralleled by a development in the type of French discourse. The increased level of specificity reflected that the relevant policymaking actors were perceived as knowledgeable interlocutors whose participation was important for the legitimacy of the new legislation, in line with V. Schmidt's model of a coordinative discourse. Thus, from the late 1980s onwards, a coordinative discourse was employed both in France and Germany.

Despite the use of coordinative discourse in both France and Germany from the late 1980s onwards, this is too weak evidence (in the presence of the stability in other elements of the sectoral state tradition) to conclude that the sectoral state traditions converged. French policymakers consistently referred to their *service public* whenever telephone policy entered public political debate, and German policymakers continued to view the state's optimal role in telecommunications policy as one of efficient manager of infrastructure provision.

Final Note

All studies have their limitations. Sectoral state traditions enable a long-term empirical comparative analysis of ideas by making it possible to operationalise these ideas, as expressed in public political discourse, and therefore requires thick descriptions and contextual exploration to be useful, qualities that do not easily fit an article format. However, the long-term investigation makes it possible to identify continuation or reoccurrence of modes of discussion and form of arguments in national sectoral debates, as exemplified by the study of French and German telephone policy debates. It is also possible to assess how new ideas, which often had their intellectual origins in other countries, are shaped by national practice and traditions.

Sectoral state traditions can therefore be a useful tool in the on-going debate about 'globalisation' as well as the broader debate on the importance of ideas in policymaking because it allows for mid-level analysis that gives sufficient scope for detail whilst ensuring coherence with known, over-arching (national or other) principles. Further research using sectoral state traditions to discuss policy convergence in a variety of geographical and sectoral settings should be able to refine the concept´s central elements and contribute to a better understanding of the qualitative differences in national policymaking.

References

Andersen, Per Dannem and Lauge Baungaard Rasmussen (2014) ´The impact of national traditions and cultures on national foresight processes´ in Futures 59, 5-17

Béland, Daniel (2009) Ideas, Institutions, and policy change in Journal of European Public Policy 16:5, 701-718

Bennett, Colin J. (1991) 'What Is Policy Convergence and What Causes It?' in *British Journal of Political Science* 21:2, 215-233

Blyth, Mark (2001) 'The Transformation of the Swedish Model. Economic Ideas, Distributional Conflict, and Institutional Change' in *World Politics* 54:1, 1-26

Campbell, John L. and Ove K. Pedersen (2014) The National Origins of Policy Ideas: Knowledge Regimes in the United States, France, Germany, and Denmark. Princeton: Princeton University

Press

Cerny, Philip G. (2000) 'Political Agency in a Globalizing World: Towards a Structurational Approach' in *European Journal of International Relations* 6:4, 435-463

Dolowitz, David P. and David March (2000) 'Learning from Abroad: The role of policy transfer in contemporary policy-making' in *Governance* 13:1, 5-24

Dyson, Kenneth (1980) The State Tradition in Western Europe, New York: Oxford University Press

Eatwell, Roger (ed.) (1997) European Political Cultures. Conflict or Convergence? London: Routledge

Elster, Jon (1989) Nuts and Bolts for the Social Sciences, Cambridge: CUP

Favell, Adrian (2001) Philosophies of Integration Basingstoke: Palgrave

Goldstein, Judith (1989) 'The Impact of Ideas on Trade Policy: The Origin of U.S. Agricultural and Manufacturing Policies' in *International Organization* 43:1, 31-71

Goldstein, J. and R.O. Keohane (1993) Ideas and Foreign Policy. Beliefs, Institutions, and Political Change, Ithaca, Cornell UP

Grimm, Dieter (1991) 'The Modern State: Continental Traditions' in Kaufmann, Franz-Xavier (ed.) The Public Sector – Challenge for Coordination and Learning, Berlin and New York: Walter de Gruyter

Hall, Peter A. (1993) 'Policy Paradigms, Social Learning, and the State' in *Comparative Politics* April, pp. 275-296

Ikenberry, John (1990) 'The International Spread of Privatization Policies: Inducements, Learning, and "Policy Bandwagoning"' in Suleiman, E. and J. Waterbury (eds) The Political Economy of Public Sector Reform and Privatization pp. 88-110

Ikenberry, John (1997) 'Patterns and Theories of the Globalization Paradigm', paper for the concurrent sessions on the 17th World Congress of IPSA, August 18-19

Jacobsen, John Kurt (1997) Dead Reckonings. Ideas, Interests and Politics in the "Information Age"', New Jersey: Humanities Press

Jenkins-Smith, H. and Paul A. Sabatier (1994) 'Evaluating the Advocacy Coalition Framework' in *Journal of Public Policy* 14:2, 175-203

Kersbergen, Kees Van and Barbara Vis (2014) <u>Comparative Welfare State Politics: Development, Opportunities, and Reform</u>. Cambridge: CUP

Kohler-Koch, Beate (2002) 'European Networks and Ideas: Changing National Policies?' European Integration Online Papers (EIoP) http://eiop.or.at/eiop/texte/2002-006.htm

Kvistad, Gregg (1999) 'The Rise and Demise of German Statism: Loyalty and Political Membership' in *European History Quartery* 30:2, 273-276

Laborde, Cécile (2000) 'The Concept of the State in British and French Political Thought' in *Political Studies* 48, 540-557

Levy, David A. L. (1997) 'Regulating Digital Broadcasting in Europe: The Limits of Policy Convergence' in *West European Politics* 20:4, 24-42

Mahnig, Hans and Andreas Wimmer (2016) ´National or convergence specificity? A typology of immigration policy in Western Europe´ in Migraciones 8, 59-99

Majone, Giandomenico (1992) 'Ideas, Interests and Policy Change', Working Paper European University Institute 1992/21

Marino, Marit Sjøvaag (2005) <u>State Traditions in Institutional Reform. A case study of French and German Telephone Policy Debates from 1876 until 1997</u>. Ph.D., London School of Economics and Political Science

Marsden, Greg and Louise Readon (2017) ´Questions of governance: Rethinking the study of transportation policy´ in Transportation Research Part A: Policy and Practice 101, 238,251

Notermans, Tom (1998) 'Policy Continuity, Policy Change, and the Power of Economic Ideas'. Arena Working Papers WP98/17. University of Oslo

Orren, Gary (1988) 'Beyond Self Interest' in Reich, Robert B. (ed.) <u>The Power of Public Ideas</u>. Cambridge, Mass: Ballinger

Peters, B. Guy (1997) 'Policy Transfers Between Governments: The Case of Administrative Reforms' in *West European Politics* 20:4, 71-88

Rochefort, David A. and Roger W. Cobb (1994) <u>The Politics of Problem Definition. Shaping the Policy Agenda</u> Lawrence: University Press of Kansas

Rohe, Karl (1993) 'The State Tradition in Germany: Continuities and Changes' in Dirk Berg-Schlosser and Ralf Rytlewski (eds) Political Culture in Germany, London: Macmillan

Sabatier, Paul A. and Hans Jenkins-Smith (1993) <u>Policy Change and Learning. An Advocacy</u>

Coalition Approach. Boulder: Westview

Sabatier, Paul A. and Edella Schlager (2000) 'Les approches cognitives des politiques publiques: perspectives américaines' in *Revue française de science politique* 50:2, 209-234

Schmidt, Vivien (2000) 'Values and Discourse in the Politics of Adjustment' in Scharpf and Schmidt (eds) Welfare and Work Vol II, Oxford, OUP

Schmidt, Vivien (2002) 'Does Discourse Matter in the Politics of Welfare State Adjustment?' in *Comparative Political Studies* 35:2, 168-193

Wilkerson, John, David Smith and Nicholas Stramp (2015) ´Tracing the Flow of Policy Ideas in Legislatures: A Text Reuse Approach´in American Journal of Political Science 59: 4, 943-956

Winkel, Georg and Sina Leipold (2016) ´Demolishing Dikes: Multiple Streams and Policy Discourse Analysis´ in Policy Studies Journal 44:1, 108-129

Wolman, Harold (1992) 'Understanding Cross National Policy Transfers: The Case of Britain and the US' in *Governance* 5:1, 27-45

Woods, Ngaire (1995) 'Economic Ideas and International Relations: Beyond Rational Neglect' in *International Studies Quarterly* 39, 161-180

Online Banking Practices in India – An Exploratory Study

Karamjeet Singh[1]

M. Saeed[2]

Harsimran Kaur[3]

[1] Panjab University, Chandigarh, India

[2] Minot State University, ND, USA

[3] GGDSD College, Chandigarh, India

ABSTRACT

Information Technology has a vital role to play in the financial sector of an economy. The banking Industry is going through a period of rapid change due to the demands of the end users and changes in technology. This study examines the customers' perception about Online banking in India. The study examines various factors including the role of government and security aspect, and suggests ways to remove customers' reluctance toward Internet banking and improve the performance of Indian banks. Descriptive and causal research methodologies were used in this study. Per the study's findings, there is a significant relationship between perception of usefulness and acceptance of Internet banking, ease of the use and acceptance of Internet banking, Trust and acceptance of Internet banking, and government policies and acceptance of Internet banking. The findings of this study have significant implications for the managers of banks who are trying to strengthen their customer base of Internet banking users.

Key Words: Customer Perception, Internet Banking, Internet Penetration, Trust, Performance Issues, Security Issues.

Introduction

The banking industry has undergone rapid technological changes and development to meet competition, challenges of technology, and the demand of the end users. Advancement in the level of technology is a key differentiator in the performance of banks (Chechen, YiJen & Tung-Heng, 2016). Indian banking sector is also poised for robust growth as the technological changes in the banking sector have brought the mobile and internet banking services to the fore. In order to enhance the overall experience of customers and to gain a competitive edge, Indian banking sector is laying greater emphasis on upgrading their technological infrastructure and on providing improved services to their clients. The financial sector is forced to engage itself to continuously search for innovative and alternative products and services to gain success. Banking sector is using internet banking as an influencing tool of value addition for attracting and retaining customers (Wilder, 2015).

In India, private and foreign banks have been the early adopters of internet banking followed by the public sector. Banking sector has started framing strategic moves directed towards enhancing value perception of the customers regarding the products/services offered by banks (Al-Shbiel & Al-Olimat, 2016). The time period of 1996-1998 can be regarded as early adoption phase for online banking practices in India as in 1996, ICCI bank took the initiative towards starting online banking services in the country. Among public sector banks, State Bank of India owns the pride of being pioneer in providing the online banking services.

With the vision to proactively encourage Online banking practices in the country, India's central bank, Reserve Bank of India took various initiatives in the eighties for the promotion of adoption of electronic payment system by offering technology based solutions. A committee was formed under the chairmanship of Dr. Rangarajan, then Governor of Reserve Bank of India, with an intention to provide cost effective alternate system. Under this committee, a plan was drawn for a five year time frame of 1985-89 for the purpose of mechanization and computerization in the banking industry of India. A second committee was then constituted for the purpose of drafting a comprehensive and detailed plan for the extension of automation to other areas of banking which led to the revolution in the banking sector. To provide legal regulation to electronic transactions and electronic commerce, the Government of India has also enacted an Act, the Information Technology Act, 2000. RBI issues several guidelines for internet banking from time to time and reviews them periodically. In India earlier the Central bank issued guideline to all the banks to take prior approval before starting any new online service but this guideline was suspended later. The banks have now been given autonomy but with a condition to ensure online services offered by banks to be covered under the provisions laid by RBI.

Banks need to look at innovation for products as well as for processes. Besides new product offerings, banks need to work towards existing products' optimization. It does not stretch one's imagination to understand that the scale and complexity of banking has undergone a tremendous change in the last 30 years. One reason is clearly the adoption of technology in banking operations such as Internet banking which has gained popularity in a very short period of time and customers are opting for Internet banking. The main advantage of Internet banking is that it reduces the lead time (i.e., in earlier times customers could spend as much as three to four hours for one banking transaction to be fully executed but now such a transaction can be done in just a few minutes). This is one reason why banks are spending more and more on technology. Internet banking is advantageous for banks and their clients. The customers become motivated through trust which plays an important role in improving the level of availability of online banking practices resulting in cost and time savings, facilitating customer's satisfaction and improvement in the status of the banks (Alsajjan and Dennis, 2010). Information technology creates and provides better services to banking industry by ensuring maximum security level (Rahman et al, 2012). Trust is also a vital consideration in internet banking in contrast with offline banking as customers are sensitive with regard to their information being shared (Suh and Han, 2003).

The services that Internet banking offers are growing due to the competitive business environment (Bruno, 2006). However, Internet banking has not been accepted by customers at the expected pace. There are many reasons that explain the slow growth of the Internet banking. Security is a main reason which results in the reluctance among customers to use Internet banking (Huang, 2007). Another is the age of the customer as often the younger generation is quicker in adopting new technologies, while older people sometimes have difficulties to adapt to those changes (Huang, 2007). Nonetheless, the Internet banking services of some banks are widely accepted while other banks are still struggling to convince customers to opt for Internet banking.

There are several factors and risks hampering the success of Internet banking:

- Cost effective delivery of services is an important factor that influences adoption of innovation by customers in the form of internet banking. The technologies must be reasonably priced relative to the alternatives. (Rothwell and Gardiner 1984).

- One rumor or wrong opinion in the market can affect any financial institution in an adverse way. This type of rumor can affect the institution no matter of the size of the bank. Internet banking has increased the probability of this type of risk (Zahorik. and Rust, 1992).

- When a bank's executives decide to go for Internet banking then the bankers should know about the risks involved in the Internet banking and should create a safe and secure Internet banking environment. Otherwise, it can affect the financial health of the company (Reibstein, 2002).

- The probability of systematic risk has increased because of the globalization effect and the integration of the world's economy (Reibstein, 2002).

- Security risk arises when someone else can get access to the exclusive data or the information about the company or its clients. This type of risk can be prevented by creating a safe and secure Internet banking environment (Reibstein, 2002).

- Lack of quality of the automated services provided by the bank impact financial performance and customer retention of a bank. (Suh and Han, 2003b).

- There are new types of risks that evolve now and then, and banking regulations may lag recognizing and controlling these new risks (Malhotra and Singh, 2006).

- The customers are concerned about their personal information and details, and lack of trust on the security issues leads to their non-adoption behavior towards internet banking (Kim et al., 2009).

- Customer retention problem in banks arises due to the lack of diffusion of Internet banking technology and it can be prevented by developing the faith in usefulness, credibility, access and speed of service. (Nasri, 2011).

- The banks are struggling to keep up with the continuous growth in IT. They are forced to work on the development of new, faster and better systems. On the other hand, they´re facing a struggle with keeping a secure service (Jarrett, 2015).

This research is intended to find answers to the above mentioned problems faced by customers and the Internet banking service providers. This research is concerned with examining Indian Internet banks, and the factors affecting the customers' acceptance of Internet banking. This research is intended to help banks and banking professionals to find factors which affect the acceptance of

Internet banking in India.

Objectives of the Study

The main objectives of this research are as follows:

- To explore the customers' perception about Internet banking in India.
- To explore the various factors affecting customers' perception toward Internet banking.
- To explore the major factors which can remove customers' reluctance toward Internet banking.
- To explore how government policies and laws affect the Internet banking sector.
- To explore the factors affecting the security of Internet banking.

Literature Review

The early version of online banking practices began in 1980s. Nottingham Building Society (NBS) introduced internet banking to NBS's customers using a platform designed by the Bank of Scotland. (Tait and Davis, 1989). NBS discontinued the services because Internet banking was not widely accepted by its customers at the time. But in the1990s, NBS and many other banking companies found success with Internet banking services as there was a rapid growth of information technology and a growing penetration of the Internet. When re-introduced in the 1990s, banking gurus thought that Internet banking would be widely used by customers for balance enquiry, banking transactions and Internet bill payment. This dream of the banking gurus was partly realized. Furst, Lang and Nolle. (2000) reported that by the end of 1990s , 88.8% of all U.S. national bank were offering online fund transfer and the balance enquiry facilities to the customers, 785 U.S. banks were offering bill payment through Internet banking, and 60% of U.S. banks were offering online loan applications. Bhatt and Bhatt (2016), Hamprecht and Brunier (2011), etc. have recognized that one of the prime objectives of the banks for introducing new and improved technologies into the banking operations is to provide superior value to the customers.

Research conducted by Pikkarainen, Pikkarainen, Karjaluoto, and Pahnila (2004) indicated that Americans have accepted Internet banking very rapidly but European countries were still the leaders in the use of the newest banking technologies especially those related to Internet banking.

Polatoglu and Ekin (2001) mentioned that since 1997 all Turkish banking companies have offered the Internet banking successfully to their customers. Also in 1990s many of these Turkish banking companies started to implement Internet banking in their respective branches. Yet, it did not prove to be a great success for all of them. Nonetheless, for banks in Turkey, Internet banking services are a compulsion as banks cannot be imagined to survive without offering Internet banking.

Seitz and Stickel (1998) outlined the many channels for which customers are able to handle their accounts. Their model suggests technical channels should be of equal value to customers. IIS (Internetstiftelsen I Sverige) statistics reveal that approximately 94% individuals use internet banking in the year 2016. Customers are not restricted to use internet banking services via computer only rather they are using devices like mobile phones, tablets via internet (IIS 2016). Uddin et al (2016) recommended that various measures should be put in place to make e-banking system smooth, effective and more secure. They concluded that e-banking has become an important phenomenon in the banking industry and it will continue as more progress and innovations are made in information technology.

Internet Banking and Security

Security is one of the reasons for the lack of interest of customers towards Internet banking. Pavlou (2001) mentioned that before the launch of the Internet banking applications even the banks were reluctant to open online banking service to customers. Factors like trust and lack of information played a crucial role in the Internet banking adoption keeping in view the security issues (Soilen, K. S., Nerme, P., Stenström, C. & Darefelt, N. 2013).

Government Policies

The growth in the field of Internet banking is accelerating and government legislation plays an important role (Lin, 2011; Afshan and Sharif, 2016). Peterson (2006) discussed such legislation. One of these laws states that banks are liable to inform customers of the new technology the bank is implementing and the risk factors associated with the technology. The bank must give the details of the last login of the account along with its associated Internet protocol (IP) address. The bank's website should provide details of all the transactions on the website. Furthermore, the legislation enforced the law that it is the liability of banks to take measures to reduce system operation and data errors. If there is any error then bank is liable for the error. Another law mandates the customers should be provided with the receipt of all the transactions and confirmed payment fund transfers (Peterson, 2006). The Turkish Government has passed legislation in which it was mentioned that banks will also be liable to protect the customer from any fraudulent activities (Peterson, 2006). This legislation recognized that customers are more vulnerable to fraudulent activities than the bank.

Perception of Usefulness

Due to high demand of Internet banking among customers there has been an explosion of the Internet based online banking applications in the market (Hong and Thong, 2013).

Beckett, Hewer and Howcroft (2000) stated that due to the demand of these types of applications, a hyper competition situation is developed in the market for the banks. Every bank is trying to provide a better and more sophisticated Internet banking experience for its customers and Internet banking has become one of the important distribution channels for banks. The success of Internet banking depends on the tailored financial products and services that fulfill the need of the customers.

Rao et. al. (2003) conducted a study on Internet banking in India and found that Indian banks offering online services still have a long way to go as compared to banks abroad. Sufficient technological infrastructure and number of users are required for online banking to be adopted in India. Beckett et al. (2000) emphasized that transaction security and transaction accuracy are also important factors which decide the success of Internet banking.

Perceived Ease of Use

In the past few years the number of the Internet banking websites has increased rapidly. Web designers think that the websites are the panacea for managing and advertising businesses, and banks should make their websites more customers interactive (Jaruwa Chirathanakul & Fink 2005). Bank websites are becoming first point of interaction with the customers. It is very important that detailed instructions and information should be provided on the website for customers to refer to. Web designers recommend that companies should use human computer interaction principle to make websites easy to understand. Customer should also be able to find the required information conveniently.

Thurow (2002) stated that in order to design a perfect website or a search engine the designer should follow these five basic rules: The site should be easy to read, easy to navigate, easy to find, consistent in layout and consistent in design. Fang He (2009), reported in his study that perceived ease of use is postulated to have a positive direct effect on attitude toward using IT. Therefore, an individual will have a positive attitude toward using a particular IT, influenced by the higher perceived use

Trust

Trust is the one factor which can prevent the growth of Internet banking services. It is a very complex and multidimensional phenomenon. For any bank that wants to implement Internet banking, it is very important to create an environment of trust among customers. The willingness to use Internet banking depends on a few factors. Some of these factors are accuracy, security, network speed, user friendliness, user involvement, and convenience.

Lee (2006) mentioned when customers do any transaction online then there is always a risk involved. Banks and Internet service providers are spending millions of dollars to secure online transactions. Yet, hackers still find new tricks to fool customers. There are many ways by which hackers try to fool customers like creating dummy websites and by providing wrong details for customers. Marketing of service is necessary in building trust among older segment (Clemes, Gan & Du (2012). Gupta, Chaturvedi, Mehta and Valeri (2000) mentioned that the information security is becoming a pivotal business and technical undertaking for any company involved in online financial activities.

In a study, it was found that the degree of trust in an electronic commerce and customers level of internet experience are positively related. Customer's experience has an effect on their tendency to trust the technology which may lead to the enhancement of their trust in the electronic commerce (Bart et al., 2005). From the above discussion, it is concluded that there is no unanimity about the factors affecting customers' perception toward Internet banking.

Methodology

The exploratory study focuses on making an analysis of online banking practices. Descriptive and causal research methodologies were used in this study. The descriptive design provided a clearer understanding of the Internet banking in India. The methodology used for this study was a survey to capture and measure the perception of the users towards Internet banking in India. The survey questions used a combination of nominal scale items, attitude rating scale items, and ordinal scale items. The background information of the respondents collected such as age, education level. Occupation, marital status helped to analyze the use pattern of online banking. The questionnaire's researchers pre-tested the survey instrument on senior colleagues who were asked for their opinions on the readability of the questions and how they would answer them.

The sample was concerned only with those aware of Internet banking in India. Hence, a convenience sample of mostly professionals from different occupations and companies were involved. Three hundred and two (302) usable surveys were collected. It was ascertained that the respondents were aware of Internet banking for personal banking uses. Therefore, the participants were able to understand and express their perceptions by answering the questionnaire honestly and meaningfully.

The dependent variable for the study was set to be the acceptance of Internet banking. The independent variables were perceived usefulness, ease of use, trust and government policies. The model adapted from Gupta (2002) uses the hypotheses that the independent variables are perceived usefulness, ease of use, trust and government policies that affect Internet banking. The following hypotheses were used.

H1: A significant relationship exists between perception of usefulness and acceptance of Internet banking.

H2: A significant relationship exists between ease of use and consumers' acceptance of Internet banking.

H3: A significant relationship exists between trust and consumers' acceptance of Internet banking.

H4: A significant relationship exists between Government policies and consumers' acceptance of Internet banking.

The hypotheses were tested using descriptive statistics, correlations, and regression methodologies. Minitab and SPSS were used to find relationships between the variables and the extent of its dependencies.

Data Analysis

The research study targeted the acceptance of Internet banking of people residing in India. The questionnaire was distributed in two ways; online using Google questionnaire and by direct interviews which resulted in 302 usable responses in total from India. Table 1 and Table 2 show the gender distribution and age distribution of the 302 respondents.

Table 1.

Gender

	Frequency	Percent
Male	162	53.64
Female	140	46.36
Total	302	100.0

Table 2.

Age

	Frequency	Percent
20-24	23	7.61
25-29	47	15.56
30-34	77	25.50
35-39	94	31.13
Above 40	61	20.20
Total	302	100.0

Table 3.

Marital Status

	Frequency	Percent
Single	124	41.06
Married	178	58.94
Total	302	100.0

Table 4.

Education

	Frequency	Percent
High school	6	1.99
Bachelor Degree	74	24.50
Master Degree	198	65.56
PHD	24	7.95
Total	302	100.0

Table 5.

Work Department

	Frequency	Percent
High school	6	1.99
Bachelor Degree	74	24.50
Master Degree	198	65.56
PHD	24	7.95
Total	302	100.0

Table 1 shows that the distribution of the respondents is almost even between males and females, with a slightly higher percentage for males (53.64 %) and the rest are females at 43.36%. Table 2 shows that the majority of the respondents were of the age group 35-39 years which is 31.13%, followed by 30-34 years age with 25.50%. Table 3 shows that from total of 302 respondents 58.94% were married and 41.06 % were single. The majority of the respondents held Master qualification at 65.56 % followed by Bachelor degree holders at 24.50 % and the lowest category was high school completers at 1.99% as shown by Table 4. Table 5 shows that the majority of the respondents were working in a finance department (40.06%) followed the administration department with 30.13 % and the marketing department at 25.17%.

Reliability Test

Each variable has undergone reliability testing before the analysis was conducted on the survey's results. Table 6 and Table 7 show the Cronbach's Alpha and item total statistics for all variables. The first four variables are independent variables, namely, perceived usefulness, perceived ease of use, trust, and government (policies). The last variable is the dependent variable, namely, acceptance of Internet banking. Results show that the variables are of high significance and have good reliability.

Table 6.

Reliability Analysis

Variable	Cronbach's Alpha	Number of Items
Perceived usefulness	0.645	5
Perceived ease of use	0.665	5
Trust	0.710	3
Government	0.660	4
Acceptance of Internet banking	0.872	4

Table 7.

Item Total Statistics

	Scale mean if item Deleted	Scale variance if item Deleted	Corrected item Total Correlation	Cronbach's Alpha if item Deleted
Perceived usefulness				
Internet banking makes it easier for me to conduct my banking transactions.	77.46	84.070	0.418	0.872
Internet banking allows me to manage my finances more efficiently.	77.56	81.290	0.530	0.869
Internet banking increases my productivity.	77.80	85.351	0.320	0.875
Internet banking made communications with banks much easier.	77.65	82.813	0.461	0.871

Overall, I believe Internet banking is more useful than traditional ways of banking.	77.45	83.298	0.427	0.872
Ease of use			
I find Internet banking easy to use.	77.69	84.234	.404	.873
Learning to use Internet banking is easy for me.	77.71	84.335	.396	.873
My interaction with internet banking is clear and understandable.	77.67	82.589	.523	.869
It is easy to get Internet banking to do what I want it to do.	77.77	81.461	.494	.870
Trust			
I trust that transaction conducted through internet banking is secure and private.	77.76	82.377	.442	.872
I trust payments made through Internet banking channel will be processed securely.	77.74	82.857	.494	.870
Government			
Government encourages and promotes the usage of Internet and e-commerce.	77.63	81.757	.451	.872
The internet infrastructure and facilities such as bandwidth is sufficient for online banking.	77.92	82.262	.451	.872
The government is driving the development of online banking.	77.75	83.712	.413	.873
The government has good regulations and laws for Internet banking.	77.90	81.529	.487	.870
Internet Banking			
Assuming that I have access to Internet banking, I intend to use it.	77.54	81.166	.579	.867
I intend to use Internet banking if the cost and time is reasonable for me.	77.44	80.872	.590	.867
I believe I will use internet banking in the future.	77.36	82.325	.485	.870
I intend to increase my use of the Internet banking in the future.	77.38	82.583	.475	.871

Regression Analysis

Table 8 shows the regression results of four models. For each model, acceptance of Internet banking is dependent variable.

Table 8:

Regression Results

Model	Variable	Adjusted R Square	Sig (F-Ratio)	Coefficient
I	Perceived usefulness	0.634	0.000	0.496
II	Perceived ease of use	0.881	0.000	1.104
II	Trust	0.689	0.000	0.367
IV	Government	0.464	0.000	0.473

For Model I the independent variable (i.e., perceived usefulness) explains the 63.4 % of the variance in the dependent variable (i.e., acceptance of Internet banking). The F-ratio shows that this model is significant. Model II significantly explains the acceptance of Internet banking and adjusted R square of 0.881 for model II shows that acceptance of internet banking is highly dependent on perceived ease of use. The F-ratio is significant for Model III. Model IV shows that government policies explain 46.4 % variation in acceptance of Internet banking and its F-ratio is significant.

Conclusion

For the exploratory study being conducted, four independent variables were identified which may affect the acceptance and growth of the Internet banking in any country. However, this particular study was set in India. The analysis shows that of four variables, two, perceived ease of use and trust, have the most significant impact on the acceptance of Internet banking. This research will help banks or Internet banking service providers find key areas in which they should concentrate in order to increase the acceptance and growth of the Internet banking market as internet banking seems poised to become an important part of the Indian banking sector in the years to come. If banks concentrate on perceived ease of use and trust then the number of the users for the Internet banking should increase. Of three independent variables, trust and usefulness are the only variables for which the banks or the Internet banking service provider can directly influence as government policies are not directly controllable by the banks. Table 9 summarizes the conclusion of the outcomes of each of the four hypotheses.

Table 9

Hypothesis and Conclusion

Hypothesis	Support	Conclusion
A significant relationship exists between perception of usefulness and acceptance of Internet banking.	Supported	The results support this hypothesis. The perception of the usefulness of Internet banking helps to promote the growth and the acceptance of Internet banking among the customers.
A significant relationship exists between ease of use and consumers' acceptance of Internet banking.	Supported	This hypothesis is supported and the result shows that acceptance of internet banking is highly dependent on perceived ease of use and concentrating on this will promote acceptance.
Significant relationship exists between trust and consumers' acceptance of Internet banking.	Supported	This hypothesis is supported as trust has a significant effect on the customer acceptance of Internet banking. Trust is a main factor which can change the perception of the customers about internet banking and promote acceptance.
A significant relationship exists between Government policies and consumers' acceptance of Internet banking.	Supported	This hypothesis is supported. Government policies affect the acceptance of internet banking. Government policy regulates Internet banking scenarios and hence prevents the customers from suffering from fraud.

Recommendations and Future Work

In the context of Internet banking in India, all the major banks in India are trying to promote online transactions in the country. According to McKinsey survey on digital banking in Asia; India is the country that leads growth in internet and mobile usage for banking. But most of the market is still untapped and there is a need to encourage and expand online banking practices by banking institutions in India to have a more sophisticated customer base.

It is important that more independent variables should be used to increase the applicability of the findings. Banks must consider training and education programs that will help customers, in particular, overcome the difficulty of using online banking as acceptance of online banking is highly dependent on perceived ease of use as per the findings of the study .As far as online banking adoption is concerned, security, trust and privacy concerns have been outlined as extremely important ones from the consumer's standpoint (Benamati and Serva 2007). With context to India, as per the findings of this study trust plays an important role, hence banks should adopt significant measures to facilitate online banking acceptance among customers by taking significant measures to maintain security of the transactions.

Besides the researched factors, there are others like attitudinal factors and system design factors which should also be considered to enhance the growth of the Internet banking in India. This study has some limitations that offer future research opportunities. This study is one that focused on India specifically. Its finding may not hold for other countries as factors (such as culture) may affect the findings. So, there is an opportunity of conducting multi-country research on the same topic. Another suggestion concerning accuracy is to target a larger sample, and to use random sampling techniques. As it was only possible to carry out a survey on a small scale as an exploratory exercise, a larger sample that includes bank customers that both used and refused to use Internet banking would be instructive.

Implications

The findings of this study have many implications for the managers of banks who are trying to strengthen their customer base of Internet banking. The main significance of this study lies in an examination of the performance of Indian banks in Internet banking services. This study has concentrated on the factors affecting the customers' acceptance of Internet bank.

This research will help the banks and banking professionals to tailor messages and operations which most effectively promote the acceptance and growth of Internet banking. First, in order to increase the growth of Internet banking (in any country) it is very important that government policies should support the Internet banking environment. The policies should be designed in such a way that they are beneficial for both customers as well as the bank. Second, trust is essential to build acceptance and use of Internet banking as is perceived usefulness. Third, facilitating ease of use is important for sustained use of Internet banking. Bankers must not only focus on employee-customer interaction issues, but on technology-customer interactions too. Ease of use means the user friendly websites with easy to follow instructions which can help the customers to perform all the functions reliably without much effort and that the website works.

References

Afshan, S. & Sharif, A. (2016). Acceptance of mobile banking framework in Pakistan. Telematics and Informatics, 33, 370-387. Retrieved from http://dx.doi.org/10.1016/j.tele.2015.09.005

Alsajjan, B. & C. Dennis (2010). Internet banking acceptance model: cross-market examination. *Journal of Business Research*, 957-963.

Al-Shbiel, N.H. Al (2016). Impact of information technology on competitive advantage in Jordanian commercial banks. Accounting information system effectiveness as a mediating variable. *International Journal of Academic Research in Accounting, Finance and Management Sciences*, 6 (3), 202-211

Bart, Y., V. Shankar, F. Sultan, & G.L. Urban (2005).Are the drivers and role of online trust the same for all web sites and consumers? A large-scale exploratory empirical study. *Journal of Marketing*, 133-152.

Beckett, A., Hewer, P., & Howcroft, B. (2000). An exposition of consumer behavior in the financial services industry. *The International Journal of Bank Marketing*, 18(1).

Benamati S. and Serva K (2007). Innovation characteristics and innovation adoption implementation: a Meta-analysis of findings. *IEEE Transaction of Engineering Management*, 29(1), 34-52.

A. Bhatt, S. Bhatt (2016). Factors affecting customers adoption of mobile banking services. *Journal of Internet Banking and Commerce*, 21 (1), 1-22

Bruno-Britz, M. (2006). The three factors for a successful online banking site. Bank Systems & Technology. Retrieved from: http://www.banktech.com/showarticle. jhtml article =186700807

Chechen, L., Yi-Jen, H. & Tung-Heng, H. (2016). Factors Influencing Internet Banking Adoption. Social Behavior & Personality: an international journal, 44(9), 1443-1455.

Clemes M. D., Gan C., & Du J. (2012). The Factors Impacting On Customers' Decisions To Adopt Internet Banking. Banks and Bank Systems, 7, pp. 33-50.

Daniel, E (1998).Online banking: Winning the majority. *Journal of Financial Services*.

Daniel, E (1999). Provision of electronic banking in the UK and the Republic of Ireland.

International Journal of Bank Marketing, 17(200), 72-82.

Fang He (1998). Decision factors for the adoption E-finance and e-commerce activities. *Journal of Internet Banking and Commerce*, 36-37.

Furst, K., Lang, W. & Nolle, D (2000). Internet banking: Developments and prospects, Office of the Comptroller of the Currency. *E&PA Working Paper*.

Gupta M., Chaturvedi A., Mehta S. & Valeri, L (2000).The experimental analysis of information security management issues for online financial services. *Paper presented at the International Conference on Information systems*, 667-675.

Gupta V. (2002).Overview of e-banking, E-banking: A Global Perspective.

M. Hamprecht, F. Brunier (2011). Enhancing the banking customer value proposition through technology-led innovation, Accenture, Zurich

Hong, W., & Thong, J. Y. (2013). Internet privacy concerns: an integrated conceptualization and four empirical studies. MIS Quarterly, 37(1), 275-298.

Huang, W. X. (2007). Institutional banking for emerging markets: Principles and practice. New York, NY: John Wiley & Sons.

Jarrett, J. E. (2015). On internet banking. Journal of Internet Banking and Commerce, 20(2), 1-4.

Jaruwa chirathanakul, B. & Fink, D (2005). Internet banking adoption strategies for a developing country, Thailand. *Internet Research*, 15(3), 295-311.

Kim, K. & B. Prabhakar (2000). Initial trust, perceived risk, and the adoption of internet banking, South Asian Journal of Management, 537-543.

Lin, H, F. (2011). An empirical investigation of mobile banking adoption: The effect of innovation attributes and knowledge-based trust. International Journal of Information Management, 31(3), 252-260.

Malhotra, P. & Singh, B (2006). The impact of Internet banking on bank's performance: The Indian experience. *South Asian Journal of Management*, 13(4), Pages 25-54.

Nasri, W (2011). Factors influencing the adoption of internet banking in Tunisia. *International Journal of Business and Management*, 116-143

Peterson, S (2006). Automating public financial management in developing countries. Faculty Research Working Paper Series, John F. Kennedy School of Government, Harvard University, Cambridge, MA.

Pikkarainen, T., Pikkarainen, K., Karjaluoto, H. & Pahnila, S (2004). Consumer acceptance of online banking: An extension of the technology acceptance model. *Journal of Internet Banking and Commerce*, 14(3).

Polatoglu V., Ekin S (2001). An empirical investigation of the Turkish consumers' acceptance of IB services. *The International Journal of Bank Marketing*, 19 (4), 156- 165.

Pavlou, P "Integrating trust in electronic commerce with the technology acceptance model: model development and validation". AMCIS Proceedings, Boston, MA, 2001

Rahman, M. H.; Uddin, N. M. and Siddique, S. A. 2012. Problems and Prospects of E-Banking in Bangladesh. International Journal of Scientific and Research Publications, 2 (7): 1-2.

Rao, G. R. and Prathima, K (2003). Internet Banking in India. *Mondaq Business Briefing*, 45-48.

Reibstein, D.J. (2002). What attracts customers to online stores, and what keeps them coming back? *Journal of the Academy of Marketing Science*, 30, 465-473.

Ribbink, D., Riel, A.C.R., Liljander, V. & Streukens S (2004). Comfort your online customer: quality trust and loyalty on the Internet. *Managing Service Quality*, 446-456.

Rothwell U. and Gardiner R (1984). Internet Banking Patronage: An empirical investigation of Malaysia. *Malaysian Journal on e-Banking*, 42(4), 57-72.

Seitz, J. & Stickel, E (1998) .Internet banking – an overview. *Journal of Internet Banking and Commerce*. Retrieved from: http://www.arraydev.com/commerce/jibc/9801-8.htm.

Soilen, K. S., Nerme, P., Stenström, C. & Darefelt, N. (2013). Usage of internet banking among different segments as an example of innovation - trust and information needs. *Journal of Internet Banking and Commerce*, 18(2), 1-7.

Suh, B. & I. Han (2003). Effect of trust on customer acceptance of Internet banking. *Electronic Commerce Research and Applications*, 247-263.

Tait, F. and Davis, R.H. (1989) .The development and future of home banking. *International Journal of Bank Marketing*, 7(2), 3-9.

Thurow S (2002). Search engine visibility. Berkley. England: New Riders, a division of Pearson Education.

Wilder, Clinton. (2015). First Internet bank opens doors. InformationWeek, 30, 28-76.

Wolfinbarger, M.F. & Gilly, M.C (2002) .COMQ: Dimensionalizing, measuring and predicting quality of the e-tailing experience. Working paper, Marketing Science Institute, Cambridge

MA, 1-51.

Zahorik, A.J. & Rust, R.T. (1992).Modeling the impact of service quality on profitability: A review", in Swartz, T.A., Bowen, D.E. and Brown, S.W. (Eds). *Advances in Services Marketing and Management*, JA Press, Greenwich, CT, 49-64.

National Comparisons of Gender Egalitarianism in Islamic-Majority and Other Countries:

An Investigation of Ethical, Social, and Economic Issues

Andy Bertsch[a]

Romie Frederick Littrell[b]

Young Seob Son[c]

[a] Minot University, ND, USA

[b] National Research University Higher School of Economics, St. Petersburg, Russian Federation

[c] Bemidji State University, USA

ABSTRACT

In this review and meta-analysis, we propose that it is unethical for a government to obstruct development of the economic ecology of its citizens. Using the participation of women in the non-agricultural work force as an indicator of utilization of economic potential, we compare three categories of Muslim-majority nations and with non-Muslim majority nations. We find that despite conditions that could indicate developing opportunities for women, their participation has declined in Muslim nations over the past ten years. We discuss explanations for this lack, and the effects on the economic development in Muslim nations.

Key Words: Economic Development, Ethics, Islamic Majority, Muslim, Nation, Women

Introduction

Syed (2008) demonstrates there is ample evidence of gender equality in the principal religious texts of Islam, the *Qur'an* and *ahadith* (admonitions traditionally attributed to the Prophet Muhammad). The *Qur'an* declares creation of men and women as a part of the divine scheme (51:49; 36:36). Syed continues that men and women possess equal rights for work and compensation. "Never will I suffer to be lost the work of any of you, be he/she male or female: you are members one of another" (3:195). Additionally, there is a large body of cross-religion, cross-cultural, and cross-national literature relating to human rights and natural law relating to employment opportunities for women; we will not approach opportunities from this point of view, but will investigate empirical indicators of the existence of discrimination against women in employment related to living in Arab-Muslim majority, non-Arab-Muslim majority, and non-Muslim majority nations. Our ethical point of view is that the government of a nation has a responsibility to maximize economic opportunity and development to benefit its citizens. There are arguments for balancing development with economic and social sustainability; while realizing their relative importance, we do not address these. Our focus is on the ethics of excluding women from the labor force as a negative effect on maximizing growth of an economy. (Some attempt to distinguish between "work force" and "labor force"; following Ross (2008) we see no reason for differentiation.) Our labor force of interest is men and women who work in non-agricultural jobs outside of the home, within the formal sector, and who are nationals of their respective country. Our focus is on the ethics of excluding women from the labor force as a negative effect on maximizing growth of an economy. Support for this position is provided in the *Qur'an* (4:75): "what has come upon you that you fight not in the cause of Allah and for the oppressed among men, women, and children who pray, 'Our Lord, take us out of this city of oppressive people...'". It follows, e.g. from Naway & Naqvi (1997), that if any harm is being done to the society or segment of society either through one's own behaviour or by that of others, then we must be moved to remedial action within the bounds of law. These and many subtler and wide-ranging issues concerning responsibilities of governments, economic development, and ethical practices are discussed in Dollery and Wallis (2001).

We present a meta-analysis of statistical data and literature for gender-related practices concerning women in business across countries. To best describe and understand women's participation in business in the Muslim world, it is first necessary to describe and understand the underlying ethnic, tribal, and cultural influences that, in some cases, pre-date the establishment of Islam. We begin by describing the nations and regions that are most affected by Islam and the underlying cultural customs. The Muslim world is vast and not homogenous (Allawi, 2009; Esposito, 2003; Triandis, 2009); there are varying denominations (e.g. Sunni, Shia, etc.) and varying schools of law (e.g. Hanafi, Shafi`i, etc.), as well as underlying societal cultures within the Muslim world which influence behaviours of the citizens and followers of Islam (see, e.g., Littrell & Bertsch, in press).

Literature Review

We first establish context. Metcalfe (2007) points out it is important to realize that interpreting societal cultural norms and organizational management and human resource practices from the Northern European and Anglo societal perspectives does not fit Islamic societies. Metcalfe has demonstrated that equality agendas do not constitute part of human resource management (HRM) policy frameworks in organizations in Islamic societies. For example, *hijab* or veiling constitutes an important aspect of a woman's professional and social identity in many Arab Islamic nations and is associated with women's empowerment. Metcalfe further suggests that we cannot understand the complexity of gender and HRM processes without connecting to broader social and economic changes relating to the rights of women in Islamic nations.

Using the World Values Survey (WVS) data, Norris and Inglehart (2002) found that citizens of Muslim societies are significantly less supportive of equal rights and opportunities for women and have significantly less permissive attitudes toward homosexuality, abortion and divorce than those living in Western, democratic countries. We find that customs and cultures, often predating the establishment of Islam, have contributed to the conservative and patriarchal orientation towards women in majority Islamic countries (Caldwell, 1982). The term *patriarchy* is used to denote the specific gender arrangements in which a wife lives with the husband's family in their residence, and individuals belong to their father's genealogical descent group (Caldwell, 1982). Kandiyoti (1988) uses "classic patriarchy" to describe gender relations and the position of women in North Africa, the Muslim Middle East (including Turkey and Iran), and South and East Asia.

Timmer & McClelland (2004) point out that the status of women in Muslim countries, as measured by employment, education, health, and political participation varies by region. The Middle East and North Africa (MENA) and South Asian have the lowest participation in the labor force. Participation in Muslim countries located in Europe, Eurasia, and East Asia are higher and nearer to that of more-developed non-Muslim countries. In the MENA, and South Asia negative discrimination concerning women is institutionalized in laws that prohibit women from participating in much of public life or fully competing in the labor market.

Korinek (2005) provides a review of evidence of micro- and macro-level studies that indicates that gender inequality inhibits long-term national economic growth, suggesting two reasons. First, better-educated women with more control over household resources have been shown to bring an increase in spending on children's education, health, and nutrition, thereby investing in future generations and the future labor force. This is particularly true in developing countries where household service help resources are relatively scarce. Second, unused female potential in terms of lower levels of education, employment, remuneration, and access to productive resources implies that the allocation of economy-wide resources is sub-optimal. Our literature review finds that the proportion of women in higher education in Muslim-majority countries is increasing, and in some cases is higher than men (Littrell & Bertsch, in press), however, this event has not led to increased participation in the non-agricultural work force, which has, in fact, been decreasing for women. For example, Metcalfe (2006) found that Arab nations strongly supported gender equality in education but not in employment. The culture supports "the development of human capabilities of women but not for their utilization" (UNDP, 2003, p. 19).

Moghadam (2008) summarizes commentary from experts who contend that for economic progress it is vital that women play a larger role in the economy and society. To varying degrees across the countries, discrimination against women is built into cultural attitudes, government policies, and legal frameworks. Family laws codify discrimination against women and girls, placing them in a position subordinate to men in the family, a practice that is then replicated in the economy and society. Korinek (2005) finds evidence that women are constrained from moving into more skilled, higher-paying jobs when trade liberalization occurs, though some studies indicate successes of some women in the region; e.g., Chamlou et al. (2007) provide an overview of somewhat isolated successes of entrepreneurial women in the MENA. McIntosh &

Islam (2010) discuss positive behaviours leading to success of women entrepreneurs in Bahrain. However, Syed, Özbilgin, Torunoglu, & Ali (2009) studying Muslim-majority implementation of *Sha'aria* and secular practice nationally find that from an institutional analysis point of view, organizations adopt practices that are considered legitimate in the eyes of their main stakeholders, even if they are not necessarily efficient.

Our samples consist of four mutually exclusive categories; see Table 1. Group 1, 'The Islamic Middle East' includes Arab nations within the Arabian Peninsula, Levant, Mashriq, and the Sinai Peninsula. These nations have a majority of Arab ethnicity, use the Arab language and script. Group 1 excludes Israel. Group 2 is the remainder of the Islamic Arab World and includes the Maghreb region of North Africa, other Arab nations on the African continent, and those societies that belong to the Arab League but are not part of Group 1. Group 3, 'The rest of the Islamic World', includes those nations not already included in Groups 1 or 2 that also have Muslim majorities (i.e., non-Arab Muslims). Group 4 is all other nations of the world and is too numerous to list here. We realize the lack of homogeneity of Group 4, but as our interest is Muslim and non-Muslim majority comparisons, the grouping is accurate enough for the purposes of this study.

Table 1.

Mutually Exclusive Country Groups

Group	Country list	
1. The Islamic Middle East : Defined as the Arabian peninsula, Levant, Mashriq, and the use of Arab language and Arab script.	Bahrain Kuwait Jordan Oman Qatar Syria Yemen	Egypt Iraq Lebanon Palestinian Territories Saudi Arabia United Arab Emirates
2. The Islamic Arab World excluding the Middle East: Defined as those nations of the Arab world not included in Group 1 including Maghreb nations and member nations of the Arab League.	Algeria Djibouti Mauritania Somalia Tunisia	Comoros Libya Morocco Sudan

3. The rest of the Islamic world: Defined as Muslim majority countries that are not of Arab ethnicity (e.g. all of Islam minus Groups 1 and 2 above).		
	Afghanistan	Albania
	Azerbaijan	Bangladesh
	Brunei	Burkina Faso
	Chad	Cyprus
	Gambia	Guinea
	Indonesia	Iran
	Kazakhstan	Kosovo
	Kyrgyzstan	Malaysia
	Maldives	Mali
	Mayotte	Niger
	Nigeria	Pakistan
	Senegal	Sierra Leone
	Tajikistan	Turkey
	Turkmenistan	Uzbekistan
4. All other nations	Too numerous to list	

Our initial research question is whether non-agricultural employment in Muslim-majority countries differs from non-Muslim countries? Our prediction is that it is lower. Additionally, do these measures differ amongst Muslim-majority countries? From prior research (Littrell & Bertsch, in press) we predict that Arab-majority Middle East countries will have lower participation, development, and opportunities for women.

We compare women's participation in the labor force in Muslim countries across three groups defined in Table 1. Our literature review indicates differences between the groups. Our review leads us to believe Group 3 countries will be similar to the developed nations of Group 4 (Timmer & McClelland, 2004, p.3) regarding women's representation in the work force. We find that women's participation in the work force is much lower in Arab than in other Muslim nations, and in non-Muslim majority nations (Littrell & Bertsch, in press). Using our categories, we will provide an overview of national indicators of hindrances, opportunities, and processes for women's participation in business in the various categorizations of Islamic nations with a comparison to non-Muslim societies.

Group 1: The Islamic Middle East

Caldwell (1982) refers to the MENA and South Asia as "the patriarchal belt". Though diverse within itself, research to date indicates the Middle Eastern countries to have generally more traditional, tribal, and conservative practices than the rest of the Islamic World. Cultures and customs of the tribal communities prevail and continue in the Middle East and the Arabian Peninsula from prior to the establishment of Islam (Al-Ahmadi, 2011; Alajmi 2001). These have contributed to a conservative and patriarchal orientation towards women for those nations in Group 1. Effendi (2003) argues that Arab cultures are patriarchal and place women in a passive role at work and in the family. Effendi states it is not Islam that places women in these roles, but rather the way that patriarchal societies interpret Islam to support their positions regarding what is and is not acceptable behaviour for women. Studies of attitudes towards women in the Arabian Gulf region generally find men are not willing to share public responsibilities with women (Abdulla, 1996), while others point out that there are contrasting views in the Arab world towards women, which reflects a deep rift in the fabric of Arab culture (Ibrahim, 1997, cited in Al Ahmadi, 2011). Ibrahim suggests that social institutions such as the family, school, and the media play a critical role in perpetuating negative values and attitudes towards women's work and role in society. These attitudes towards women are not unique to the Arab world; but are quite ingrained in day-to-day opinions, attitudes, beliefs, and behaviours in that region.

Group 2: The Islamic Arab World (excluding the Middle East)

Arab populations encompass a vast geographical region that extends from Iraq in the east to Morocco in the west. They occupy the whole of traditional Mesopotamia, the Middle East, the Arabian Gulf, North Africa, as well as parts of East and West Africa. Arab populations are distributed in 23 different countries: Algeria, Bahrain, Comoros, Djibouti, Egypt, Eritrea, Iraq, Jordan, Kuwait, Lebanon, Libya, Mauritania, Morocco, Oman, Palestine, Qatar, Saudi Arabia, Somalia, Sudan, Syria, Tunisia, United Arab Emirates, and Yemen. Arabs do not homogeneously populate this geographical area and tend to be concentrated in narrow locations such as in the Nile, Euphrates, and Tigris valleys, the coastal regions of North Africa, the Gulf, and Western Asia.

From the WVS Inglehart & Welzel (2010) find that the countries in our Group 2 are very similar as a well-defined high Traditional / low Secular-Rational, high Survival / low Self-Expression values region. Schwartz (2006) found the group to have similar individual values, with high Embeddedness and low Affective Autonomy and Intellectual Autonomy, and very high Conservatism (Schwartz, 1999). Minkov (2011, discussed in Littrell, 2012) also found this group to be culturally similar to one another.

Group 3: The rest of the Islamic world (non-Arab Islamic majority)

For Group 3, Rizzo, Abdel-Latif & Meyer (2007) find that in non-Arab Muslim countries there are higher levels of support for women's rights compared to Arab Muslim countries. Whilst the countries in the group are geographically and culturally diverse, they all fall in Caldwell's *Patriarchal Belt*.

The majority of the countries from the 1999–2003 wave of the WVS are part of the band of "classic patriarchy" that extends from North Africa, through the Muslim Middle East to South and East Asia, particularly India and China, and cuts across the cultural and religious traditions of Hinduism, Confucianism and Islam (see Kandiyoti, 1988 for a more in depth discussion). This zone is characterized by the low status of women in general as a result of patrilineal-patrilocal households, high fertility rates coupled with low age at first marriage, high maternal and infant mortality rates, higher rates of female illiteracy, lower levels of female educational enrollment, low female labor force participation, and the lack of women's political participation and political rights (Moghadam, 2003 & 1993).

Group 4: All other nations

The defining characteristic of the countries in Group 4 is that they do not have Muslim-majority populations. Other than that they maximize global cultural and geographical diversity. This group does include India and China with traditions of Hinduism and Confucianism, being well-established members of the Patriarchal Belt (Caldwell, 1983, and Kandiyoti, 1988).

Knowledge as a Factor of Production

The addition of "knowledge" as a factor of economic production has been suggested of significant importance in creating new wealth within a society (see, e.g., Powell & Snellman (2004), Stam (2007), and Syverson (2011)). Knowledge has long been identified as an important component of production and an engine of economic growth throughout history; all economic growth has had a knowledge component (see, e.g., Machlup, 1962/1973; Toffler, 1980; OECD, 1996). In a knowledge-based economy human capital (the skills and education of its people) is a crucial factor to achieve sustained long term growth and a key determinant of a society's economic competitiveness. The World Economic Forum's (WEF) Global Gender Gap Index of

2011 (Hausman et al., 2011) shows a strong correlation of knowledge indicators with global competitiveness and GDP per capita (GDPpc). As an indicator, the trends of high-technology exports of the Arab World significantly lag behind those of North America and OECD members (World Bank, 2012).

According to the WEF's Global Gender Gap Index 2011 the overall gender gap index score of the MENA region is approximately 58%. This region comes in last amongst six regional categories. MENA also is in last place for the economic participation and opportunity scores. The report describes countries in the region as having made substantial investment to reduce the gender gap in education yet the gender gap in economic opportunity remains the widest in the world. As women account for half of the world's population and half of its talent, the economic cost of not developing or not using this talent looms huge (Bertsch & Warner-Søderholm, 2012). Closing gender gaps and utilizing the potentials of women can be keys to enhanced productivity and economic growth. Excluding half of a country's population from accumulation of knowledge and generation of wealth retards economic growth.

Methods

This article is an exploratory survey and review of extant public data sources; we are seeking to explore and define relationships as well as interpret indicative results. We are discussing the relationships, if any, among societal-level variables of (i) investment in knowledge creation, (ii) gender egalitarianism in employment outside of the home in non-agricultural industries, and (iii) the prevalence and impact of knowledge industries on overall GDP. We find from our literature review that these are inadequately explored relationships. Our data are from public sources where usable data is available, hence convenience samples, a reasonable and acceptable process in exploratory research, are used herein (Hair, Babin, Money, & Samouel, 2003; Malhotra, 2007; and Zikmund & Babin, 2007).

Our methodology is to explore relationships between observable investment in the development of human capital, gender-based employment in non-agricultural business sectors, and the impact that knowledge sectors have on societal GDP. Our method includes furcating societal level data into the four mutually exclusive groups in Table 1.

Data Sources

The UN Statistics Division (UNSD; UN, 2000; World Bank, 2011) collects and publishes data tracking the "Share of women in wage employment in the non-agricultural sector" across the world, and has been collecting this data, along with other data elements, since 1990.

The World Bank publishes a Data Catalog of over 8,000 indicators from 18 different categories. Of particular interest to us is the Science and Technology indicator titled "High-technology exports (% of manufactured exports)". High-technology exports are products with high R&D intensity, such as in aerospace, computers, pharmaceuticals, scientific instruments, and electrical machinery (Worldbank.org, n.d.a).

The Skills & Innovation Policy (SIP) program of the World Bank Institute's Growth and Crisis practice provides advice on four Knowledge Economy (KE) indicators: (i) economic and institutional regime, (ii) education, (iii) innovation, and (iv) information and communication technologies (ICTs). The Knowledge Assessment Methodology (KAM) is a set of 148 structural and qualitative variables to measure and index countries in the four KE indicators, which are then aggregated into two overlapping indices. First, the Knowledge Index (KI) measures a country's ability to generate, adopt and diffuse knowledge. This is an indication of the overall potential of knowledge development in a given country (Worldbank.org, n.d.b). The second index is the Knowledge Economy Index (KEI) which takes into account whether the environment is conducive for knowledge to be used effectively for economic development. The KEI represents the overall level of development of a country or region towards the Knowledge Economy.

The World Bank also publishes various economic and social indicators. Of interest to us were the percentages of total GDP attributable to both services and industry, as defined in the International Standard Industrial Classification (UNSTATS.UN.ORG, 2012).

Analysis

We limit our analyses to correspond with the period since the UN's Millennium Development

Goals were established and where data is available, representing a time frame where the global array of nations have agreed to engage in improving the lot of women in their countries. Our analyses included the average share of women who are employed in the non-agricultural sector since the year 2000; the average share of high-technology exports as a percentage of total exports; the average Knowledge Economy Index (KEI); the average Knowledge Index (KI); the average percentage of services as a share of total GDP; and the average percentage of industry as a share of GDP across the four societal groupings described earlier.

Share of women in wage employment in non-agricultural sectors

Using the UNSD data for "Share of women in wage employment in the non-agricultural sector", averages were calculated for the period of 2000 to the most recent reported period. Table 2 illustrates those averages, standard deviations, and the results of two-sample t-tests with unequal sample sizes and non-homogenous variances for each of the country groups.

Table 2

Means, standard deviations, and t-tests for average share of women employed in non-agricultural sectors across groups

Probability Values	The Islamic Middle East Mean = 15.48% SD = 4.23	The Islamic Arab World excluding the Middle East Mean = 23.29% SD = 5.57	The rest of the Islamic world Mean = 30.65% SD = 12.2
The Islamic Arab World excluding the Middle East Mean = 23.29% SD = 5.57	t = 2.26 p < 0.05		
The rest of the Islamic world Mean = 30.65% SD = 12.2	t = 5.51 p < 0.001	t = 1.86 p < 0.05	
All Other Nations Mean = 41.91% SD = 6.27	t = 16.76 p < 0.001	t = 5.74 p < 0.001	t = 4.54 p < 0.001

All Muslim-majority groups have a lower rate of employment compared to "All Other Nations". "The Islamic Middle East" has a lower rate of female participation in non-agricultural sectors compared to "The Islamic Arab World excluding the Middle East" (t=2.26, p<0.05); "The rest of the Islamic world" (t=5.51, p<0.001); and "All Other Nations" (t=16.76, p<0.05). The analyses indicate that the employment rate of women in the Islamic Middle East is significantly lower than the other three categories.

"The Islamic Arab World excluding the Middle East" countries have a lower rate of female participation in the non-agricultural sectors compared to "The rest of the Islamic world" ($t=1.86$, $p<0.05$) and "All Other Nations" ($t=5.74$, $p<0.001$). The analyses indicate that the employment rate of women in the Islamic Arab World excluding the Middle East is significantly lower than the non-Arab Muslim world and all other nations.

Finally, "The rest of the Islamic world" is found to have a lower rate of female participation in the non-agricultural sectors compared to "All Other Nations" ($t=4.54$, $p<0.001$). The analyses indicate that the employment rate of women in the non-Arab Muslim world is significantly lower than all non-Muslim nations.

Average of high-tech exports as a percentage of all manufactured exports

High-technology exports are products with high R&D intensity, such as in aerospace, computers, pharmaceuticals, scientific instruments, and electrical machinery. Table 3 illustrates the average of high-tech exports as a percentage of all manufactured exports, standard deviations, and the two-sample t-tests for all four groups.

Table 3.

Means, standard deviations, and t-tests for of high tech exports as a percentage of all manufactured exports across groups, 2000 to present

Probability Values	The Islamic Middle East Mean = 1.07% SD = 1.803	The Islamic Arab World excluding the Middle East Mean = 4.21% SD = 5.87	The rest of the Islamic world Mean = 10.08% SD = 13.06
The Islamic Arab World excluding the Middle East Mean = 4.21% SD = 5.87	t = 2.27 p < 0.05		
The rest of the Islamic world Mean = 10.08% SD = 13.06	t = 3.16 p < 0.01	t = 1.87 p < 0.05	
All Other Nations Mean = 10.49% SD = 13.07	t = 8.54 p < 0.001	t = 3.69 p < 0.01	t = 0.14 Not significant

From Table 3, we find that Group 1 has a significantly lower average of high-technology exports as a percentage of all manufactured exports compared to Group 2 (t=2.27, p<0.05), Group 3 (t=3.16, p<0.01), and Group 4 (t=8.54, p<0.001). Further, we find that Group 2 has significantly lower high-tech exports compared to Group 3 (t=1.87, p<0.05) and Group 4 (t= 3.69, p<0.01). Lastly, we find that Group 3 has no significant difference in high-tech exports compared to Group 4.

Knowledge Index

The Knowledge Index (KI) measures a country's ability to generate, adopt, and diffuse knowledge. This is an indication of the overall potential of knowledge development in a given country. The Knowledge Index does not measure a country's realization of a Knowledge Economy. Table 4 illustrates the averages of the Knowledge Index, standard deviations, and two-sample t-tests for each of the country groups.

Table 4.

Means, standard deviations, and t-tests for averages of Knowledge Index for each of the country groups

Probability Values	The Islamic Middle East Mean = 4.92 SD = 1.68	The Islamic Arab World excluding the Middle East Mean = 2.81 SD = 1.53	The rest of the Islamic world Mean = 3.45 SD = 1.94
The Islamic Arab World excluding the Middle East Mean = 2.81 SD = 1.53	t = 2.63 p < 0.05		
The rest of the Islamic world Mean = 3.45 SD = 1.94	t = 2.15 p < 0.05	t = 0.83 Not significant	
All Other Nations Mean = 5.44 SD = 2.59	t = 0.92 Not significant	t = 3.92 p < 0.01	t = 3.81 p < 0.001

Group 1 has a significantly higher Knowledge Index than Group 2 (t=2.63, p<0.05) and Group 3 (t=2.12, p<0.05) while there is no significant difference between Group 1 and Group 4 in the KI means. There is no significant difference between Group 2 and Group 3 in the KI means; however, Group 2 has a significantly lower Knowledge Index than Group 4 (t=3.92, p<0.01). Similarly, Group 3 has a significantly lower Knowledge Index than Group 4 (t=3.81, p<0.001). Although the KI mean scores for Group 1 and Group 4 were not deemed to be significantly different, we must remember that the KI scores reveal a country's *potential* for knowledge development. Recall that the WEF's Global Gender Gap Index 2011 describes countries in the MENA (e.g. the Arab Muslim world) as having made substantial investment to reduce the gender gap in education yet the gender gap in economic opportunity remains the widest in the world.

Knowledge Economy Index

The Knowledge Economy Index (KEI) takes into account whether the environment is conducive for knowledge to be used effectively for economic development. It is an aggregate index that represents the overall level of development of a country or region towards the Knowledge Economy. Table 5 illustrates the averages of KEI, standard deviations, and two sample t-tests for each of the country groups.

Table 5.

Means, standard deviations, and t-tests for averages of KEI across each of the country groups

Probability Values	The Islamic Middle East Mean = 5.01 SD = 1.63	The Islamic Arab World excluding the Middle East Mean = 2.74 SD = 1.41	The rest of the Islamic world Mean = 3.39 SD = 1.80
The Islamic Arab World excluding the Middle East Mean = 2.74 SD = 1.41	t = 3.00 p < 0.01		
The rest of the Islamic world Mean = 3.39 SD = 1.80	t = 2.49 p < 0.05	t = 0.91 Not significant	
All Other Nations Mean = 5.45 SD = 2.55	t = 0.80 Not significant	t = 4.33 p < 0.01	t = 4.19 p < 0.001

We find that Group 1 has a significantly higher KEI average than Group 2 (t=3.00, p<0.01) and Group 3 (t=2.49, p<0.05) but no significant difference when compared to Group 4. Group 2 has no significant difference in the KEI mean compared to Group 3, Group 2 did have a significantly lower KEI mean than Group 4 (t=4.33, p<0.01). Lastly, Group 3 has a significantly lower KEI mean than Group 4 (t=4.19, p<0.001).

The KI mean scores reported earlier indicate a country's *potential* for knowledge development. The KEI score takes into account whether the environment is conducive for knowledge to be used effectively for economic development. Taken together the KI and KEI scores would indicate that the Middle East has both the potential and supportive environment for knowledge development. However, as stressed earlier, the WEF's Global Gender Gap Index 2011 reports the MENA to be in last place among six regional categories in economic participation and opportunity scores.

Even though there is no significant difference between Group 1 and Group 4 in terms of KI and KEI mean scores, the gender gap persists. We believe this may be attributable to the economic structure of Group 1 (Drucker, 1993; Toffler, 1980) and the presence of an oil-based economy (Ross, 2008). We will reserve discussion of Ross's argument applied to Group 1 until after we explore the economic structure of the four groups.

Drucker (1993) and Toffler (1980) suggest that economic development will progress from industrial-based to knowledge-based in which the competitive advantage of organizations is based on the ability to exploit knowledge resources. The transition to the knowledge economy focuses on the increase in scale of knowledge as a production factor (Stam, 2007). To explore this, our analyses will now include the percentage of the GDP that relies on services vs. industry in the four groups.

Percentage of GDP attributable to services

Sidani (2005) discussing women's employment in Arab Muslim societies finds that the majority of women who do work outside the home are in educating females, nursing, and medical care. Women also deliver female-oriented retail and personal care services. To investigate the impact of this phenomenon, we calculated the percentages of total GDP attributable to services as defined by the World Bank for the four groups. Table 6 illustrates the percentage of GDP attributable to services, the standard deviations, and two sample t-tests for the four groups.

Table 6.

Means, standard deviations, and t-tests for services as a percentage of total GDP averaged from 2000 to present

Probability Values	The Islamic Middle East Mean = 46.78% SD = 14.31	The Islamic Arab World excluding the Middle East Mean = 46.06% SD = 16.02	The rest of the Islamic world Mean = 46.68% SD = 13.44
The Islamic Arab World excluding the Middle East Mean = 46.06% SD = 16.02	t = 0.09 not significant		
The rest of the Islamic world Mean = 46.68% SD = 13.44	t = 0.02 not significant	t = 0.09 not significant	
All Other Nations Mean = 58.26% SD = 14.67	t = 2.26 $p < 0.05$	t = 1.86 $p < 0.05$	t = 4.05 $p < 0.001$

Each of the three Muslim categories has statistically lower means than "All Other Nations". Our review indicates the situation for women in Muslim-majority countries is that their participation in work appears to be generally limited to service industries, which are a smaller portion of the national economies than in the non-Muslim-majority countries.

Some good news for the situation is that we also found that the percentage of GDP attributable to services (ISIC divisions 50-99) has been increasing steadily in recent years across the globe. In general, an economy that is turning toward a knowledge-based economy will increase the proportion of services in GDP.

Percentage of GDP attributable to industry

The percentages of total GDP attributable to non-service industry as defined by the World Bank were then calculated for the four groups. Table 7 illustrates the percentage of GDP attributable to industry, the standard deviations, and the two sample t-tests across each of the country groups.

Table 7.

Means, standard deviations, and t-tests for industry as a percentage of total GDP averaged from 2000 to present

Probability Values	The Islamic Middle East Mean = 45.91% SD = 14.96	The Islamic Arab World excluding the Middle East Mean = 35.01% SD = 18.75	The rest of the Islamic world Mean = 31.72% SD = 13.91
The Islamic Arab World excluding the Middle East Mean = 35.01% SD = 18.75	t = 1.20 not significant		
The rest of the Islamic world Mean = 31.72% SD = 13.91	t = 2.45 p < 0.05	t = 0.42 not significant	
All Other Nations Mean = 28.32% SD = 12.62	t = 3.30 p < 0.01	t = 0.88 not significant	t = 1.23 not significant

The Islamic Middle East has a significantly higher percentage of GDP attributable to industry when compared to all non-Arab Muslim countries (t=2.45, p<0.05) and all non-Muslim countries (t=3.30, p<0.01). No other mean differences were significant. Hence we find that in the Muslim-majority MENA region, a large portion of available jobs appears to not be open to women. Opposite of that we found in the analysis of trends in services, we found the percentage of GDP attributable to industry (ISIC divisions 10-45) has had a steadily decreasing trend globally.

Yet Another Detriment to Women's Employment in the Middle East: Expanding Oil Production in the 1960s and 1970s

The Oil Revolution of the 1960s and 1970s may have been another negative turning point for the treatment of women in the Middle East. We have discussed that it is not so much the original Islamic writings in the Qur'an or even the fatwa that have been decreed over the years but traditional patriarchal society. Ross (2008) proposed a demarcation in the treatment of women in the Middle East and the Arab world in general is the wealth derived by oil production in the region. As a society enjoys revenues from oil and gas production, females experience lower participation rates in the labor force.

Ross (2008) suggested gender egalitarianism in the Muslim World, particularly in the Middle East and parts of North Africa, has relatively little to do with Islam but much to do with the region's oil-based economy. Different economic growth patterns bring different gender relationships. According to Ross, when growth (the economic growth based on the export-oriented manufacturing and agriculture) encourages women to join the formal labor market, it ultimately brings about greater gender equality; when growth is based on oil and mineral extraction, it prevents women from entering the labor force and tends to exaggerate gender inequalities.

Ross (2008) tested two hypotheses. The first is that a rise in the value of oil production will reduce female participation in the labor force. The second is that a rise in the value of oil production will reduce female political influence. His results were consistent with both statements and confirmed there is a strong correlation between female labor force participation and female political influence. In short, oil not only hinders democracy; it also hinders more equitable gender relations.

Although females have experienced a significant increase in education and literacy (compared to men) since 1970, women have not been so fortunate in the realms of economic advancement or political representation. For example, Freedom House has been producing a Freedom in the World Index since 1973. This index includes political rights and civil liberties. Making up the civil liberties portion of the index includes such benchmarks as autonomy, social freedoms, and gender equality. Although the index does not pre-date the Oil Revolution, one finds interesting trends from 1973 onward. For example, Arab Muslim countries such as Bahrain, Egypt, Iraq, Kuwait, Libya, and Syria experienced trends toward more freedom for three to seven year beginning in 1973 followed by a prolonged move toward the "not free" designation by Freedom House. On the other hand, non-Arab Muslim nations experienced on average a slow but steady pace toward freedom during the same period with non-Arab nations such as Bangladesh, Burkina Faso, Chad, Nigeria, Senegal, and Turkey setting the pace toward more civil freedoms (www.freedomhouse.org).

When controlled for religion and regional culture, the relationship between oil and gas production and revenue as a corollary to women's participation in the labor force holds. For example, in the Middle Eastern Arab societies (Arab, Islamic, and geographically bound by the Arabian Peninsula), as oil and gas economic rents increased, the percentage of women participating in the workforce decreased.

Discussion and Conclusions

In summary, experts contend that for women to play a larger role in the economy and society is vital to the region's progress (Moghadam, 2008). Women in Islamic majority countries still face gender discrimination that prevents them from reaching their potential, despite impressive gains in education. To varying degrees across the countries, discrimination against women is built into cultural attitudes, government policies and legal frameworks. Family laws codify discrimination against women and girls, placing them in a position subordinate to men in the family, a practice that is then replicated in the economy and society. There is evidence that women are constrained from moving into more skilled, higher-paying jobs when trade liberalization occurs because they have less access to resources, education and time (Korinek, 2005). This represents one extreme of discrimination in women's employment opportunities.

In our literature review we present previous research findings indicating participation of women in the non-agricultural labor force is necessary to increase the rate of economic advancement in a nation. Our findings indicate significant gains can be achieved in knowledge-based aspects of an economy, an area where women could easily be included. We also find evidence supporting suppression of women's participation in Muslim-majority nations, especially in the Middle East.

In our analyses we demonstrate that from publically available national statistical data:

1. The Islamic Middle East countries have the lowest percentage of participation of women in the labor force, other Islamic Arab nations are next lowest, the rest of the Islamic world next lowest, and the "all other nations group" the highest. All differences between adjacent groups are significant at $p<0.05$ or stronger.

2. Our literature review leads us to believe that women can more successfully participate in service industries than in industrial-manufacturing. We find that the MENA region has the lowest percentage of businesses in the service sector, the rest of the Islamic world next and significantly higher, and "all other nations" significantly higher than any of the Muslim-majority groups. The obvious implication, and one supported by analyses, is that Muslim-majority nations have a larger proportion of their economies in the industrial sectors, with fewer jobs appropriate for women.

3. We review Ross (2008), who provides convincing evidence that in countries where economic wealth is derived from oil production, females experience lower participation in the labor force in general. We do not explore the socio-economic reasons in this paper.

We conclude that living in a Muslim-majority nation retards participation of women in the non-agricultural labor sector. Evidence indicates that this is due more to the total overlap of Muslim-majority nations and the *Patriarchal Belt* than to Islamic tenets in government and society, with societal tenets taking precedence over Islamic tenets. Nonetheless, nations that do not have Islamic majorities tend to fare significantly better in participation of women in the labor force compared to all our categories of Islamic-majority nations.

Metcalfe (2008) finds that Arab states are committed to social change and reform, but within the framework of an Islamic gender order. This will require separation of the multi-thousand years of patriarchal culture in the belt and the intents of the *Qur'an* and *ahadith*. There are grassroots organisations promoting women's advancement and empowerment through raising literacy levels, making provisions for business programmes as well as supporting entrepreneurial development. To ensure women's economic security, there is a need for an enabling institutional, legal and regulatory framework to facilitate women's access to economic resources. This will require some of the women's administrative bodies in Arab states to give equal emphasis to the work as well as the private sphere. Metcalfe (2011) proposes some national and business organisational policies that should be of interest to governments and businesses in Muslim-majority nations for moving their economic and social development forward in the 21st century through greater participation of women in business. On the other hand, Syed (2008) argues that the concepts of equal opportunity and concerns about diversity are generally indigenous to Anglo-Western contexts and implementation in Muslim majority countries must be customized according to local socio-cultural contexts. A non-local discourse on diversity management faces the traditional challenges of local non-compatibility (Jones et al. 2000). Based on the history and origins of management research, the extant management knowledge is far from global. It is, therefore, important to contextually locate the multilevel discourse of gender and diversity management and its enactment within the unique context of each society. And, after all, Syed & Kramar (2009) note that the Western approach has not achieved equitable employment outcomes for women nor for other diverse employees in Western countries. So we are discussing issues of degree. Accommodating diversity may require accommodating differences that may prevent equality. It is, therefore, important to properly situate the multilevel discourse of diversity management and its enactment within the unique context of each society.

Shortcomings and Future Directions in Research

Our study clearly demonstrates the differences we proposed in our tests, but we are slightly confined by publishing deadlines. We plan further exploration of this kind of issue with a more finely parsed set of categories within the Patriarchal Belt, and general influences of a majority of the population in a country adhering to the same religion. Ross (2008) provides insight into the possibility that the source of wealth of a nation may influence societal and institutional gender relations, and investigations of sources other than oil are called for. Difficulties in access to individuals for societal studies, particularly women, have been in place in the past. Ways need to be found to remedy this lack of access to produce valid studies at various levels of analysis.

References

Norris, P. and R. Inglehart (2002) Islamic culture and democracy: Testing the "clash of civilizations" thesis, *Comparative Sociology*, 1, 235–63.

United Nations Development Programme (UNDP). (2003). *Arab Human Development Report.* New York, NYUSA: United Nations Publications.

Worldbank.org. (2011), World Development Indicators. http://data.worldbank.org/data-catalog/world-development-indicators, accessed 27 May 2012.

Abdulla, I. (1996), "Attitudes towards women in the Arabian Gulf region", *Women in Management Review*, 11(1), 29–39.

Al-Ahmadi, Hanan. (2011). Challenges facing women leaders in Saudi Arabia, *Human Resource Development International*, 14(2), 149-166.

Alajmi, A. (2001), Factors that support Arab Muslim women in their career roles, PhD dissertation, University of Pittsburgh, Pittsburgh, PA, USA, Ann Arbor, MIUSA: ProQuest Theses & Dissertations.

Allawi, A.A. (2009) *The crisis of Islamic civilization.* New Haven, CTUSA: Yale University Press.

Bertsch, A. & Warner-Søderholm, G. (2012) Updating Cross Cultural Management: Exploring the Relationships between Cultural Values and Gender Inequality Practices, Online Proceedings Academy of International Business Annual Conference 2012, Washington, D.C., Session 2.4.13.

Caldwell, John C. (1982). *Theory of fertility decline*, London, UK: Academic Press.

Chamlou, Nadereh, & World Bank Staff & Consultants. (2007). *The Environment for women's entrepreneurship in the Middle East and North Africa Region.* Washington, DCUSA: The World Bank, http://web.worldbank.org/WBSITE/EXTERNAL/COUNTRIES/MENAEXT/0,,content MDK:21517656~pagePK:146736~piPK:146830~theSitePK:256299,00.html

Dollery, Brian & Wallis, Joe. (2001). *The theory of market failure and policy making in contemporary local government.* Working Paper Series in Economics No. 2001-6, University of New England, Arimidale, NSW, Australia, available at http://www.une.edu.au/febl/EconStud/wps.htm

Drucker, P. (1993). *Post-capitalist society*, London, UK: HarperCollins.

Effendi, A. (2003). *Enable workers: An introduction to the improvement and continuous development*, Riyadh, Saudi Arabia: IPA, The Arab Organization for Administrative Development.

Esposito, J. L. (2003). *Unholy war: Terror in the name of Islam*. New York, NYUSA: Oxford Press.

Hair, J. F., Jr., Babin, B., Money, A. H., & Samouel, P. (2003), *Essentials of business research methods*. Wiley, New York, NY, USA.

Hausmann, R., Tyson, L., Bekhouche, Y., & Zahidi, S. (2011), *The Global Gender Gap Index 2011*, Geneva, Switzerland: World Economic Forum.

Ibrahim, A. (1997). Arab women leaders and sustainable development problems and constraints. Submitted in the *First Annual Conference of Arab Women Leaders and Sustainable Development*, Alexandria, Egypt.

Inglehart, R. & Welzel, C. (2010). Changing Mass Priorities: The Link between Modernization and Democracy. *Perspectives on Politics*, 8(2), 551-567.

Kandiyoti, D. (1988). Bargaining with patriarchy. *Gender and Society*, 2(3), 274–90

Korinek, J. (2005). *Trade and gender: issues and interactions*, OECD Trade Policy Working Paper No. 24, Publications Service, Paris, France: OECD.

Littrell, R.F. & Bertsch, A. (in press) U.N. Millennium Development Goals and gender equality in employment in the Middle East, *Foresight: The journal of future studies, strategic thinking and policy*, (Prepublication proof available in academic commons at http://crossculturalcentre.homestead.com/WorkingPapers.html).

Littrell, Romie F. (2012). Clustering national cultures: A fallacy, or not, or not always? *Proceedings Academy of International Business 2012 Annual Meeting*, Washington, DC, USA, June 30-July 3, 2012, East Lansing, MIUSA: MSU-CIBER & Eli Brad College of Business at Michigan State University.

Machlup, Fritz. (1962/1973). *The production and distribution of knowledge in the United States*. Princeton, NJUSA: Princeton University Press.

Malhotra, N. K. (2007). *Marketing research: An applied orientation, 5th ed.,* Upper Saddle River, NJUSA: Pearson Prentice Hall.

McIntosh, John C. & Islam, Samia. (2010). Beyond the Veil: The Influence of Islam on Female Entrepreneurship in a Conservative Muslim Context, *International Management Review*, 6(1): 103-109.

Metcalfe, Beverly Dawn. (2006). Exploring cultural dimensions of gender and management in the Middle East , *Thunderbird International Business Review*, 48(1), 93–107.

Metcalfe, Beverly Dawn. (2007). Gender and human resource management in the Middle East, *International Journal of Human Resource Management*, 18(1), 54–74.

Metcalfe, Beverly Dawn. (2008). Women, management and globalization in the Middle East, Journal of Business Ethics, 83, 85–100.

Metcalfe, Beverly Dawn. (2011). Women, work organization, and social change: human resource development in Arab Gulf States, *Human Resource Development International*, 14(2), 123-129.

Minkov, Michael. (2011). *Cultural Differences in a Globalizing World*, Bingley, UK: Emerald Publishing Group Ltd.

Moghadam, V.M. (2008). Feminism, legal reform and women's empowerment in the Middle East and North Africa, *International Social Science Journal*, Vol. 59 No. 191, pp. 9-16.

Naway, Syed & Naqvi, Haider. (1997). The dimensions of an Islamic economic model, *Islamic Economic Studies*, 4(2), 1-23.

OECD (1996), *The Knowledge-Based Economy*, Paris, France: OECD.

Powell, W. W., & Snellman, K. (2004) The knowledge economy, *Annual Review of Sociology*, 30, 199-220.

Rizzo, Helen; Abdel-Latif, Abdel-Hamid & Meyer, Katherine. (2007). The Relationship Between Gender Equality and Democracy: A Comparison of Arab Versus Non-Arab Muslim Societies, *Sociology*, 41(6), 1151–1170.

Ross, Michael L. (2008). Oil, Islam, and women, *American Political Science Review*, 102(1), 107-123.

Schwartz, S. H. (1999) A Theory of Cultural Values and Some Implications for Work, *Applied Psychology: An International Review*, 1999, 48 (1), 23–47

Schwartz, S. H. (2006). A Theory of Cultural Value Orientations: Explication and Applications. *Comparative Sociology*, 5(2/3), 137-182.

Sidani, Yusuf. (2005). Women, work, and Islam in Arab societies, *Women in Management Review*, Vol. 20 No. 7, pp. 498-512.

Stam, C. (2007) Knowledge Productivity: Designing and testing a method to diagnose knowledge productivity and plan for enhancement, Doctoral thesis, University of Twente, Enschede, The Netherlands.

Syed, Jawad. (2008). A context-specific perspective of equal employment opportunity in Islamic societies. *Asia Pacific Journal of Management*, 25(2), 135-151.

Syed, Jawad & Özbilgin, Mustafa. (2009). A relational framework for international transfer of diversity management practices, *The International Journal of Human Resource Management*, 20(12), 2435–2453.

Syed, Jawad; Özbilgin, Mustafa; Torunoglu, Dilek & Ali, Faiza. (2009). Rescuing gender equality from the false dichotomies of secularism versus Shariah in Muslim majority countries, *Women's Studies International Forum*, 32(2), 67-79.

Syverson, C. (2011) What Determines Productivity*?, Journal of Economic Literature*, 49:2, 326–365.

Timmer, Peter & McClelland, Donald. (2004). Economic growth in the Muslim world: How can USAID help?" U.S. Agency for International Development, Washington, DC, USA.

Toffler, A. (1980). *The Third Wave*, New York, NY: Bantum Books.

Triandis, H. C. (2009). *Fooling ourselves: Self-deception in politics, religion, and terrorism*, Westport CT: Praeger.

United Nations. (2000), *United Nations Millennium Declaration (United Nations General Assembly Resolution 55/2)*, United Nations, New York, NY, www.un.org/milleennium/declaration/ares552e.pdf.

UNSTATS.UN.ORG. (2012). Detailed structure and explanatory notes ISIC Rev.4 (International Standard Industrial Classification of All Economic Activities, Rev.4), http://unstats.un.org/unsd/cr/registry/regcst.asp?Cl=27, accessed 27 May 2012.

World Bank (2012), Knowledge Assessment Methodology 2012, http://go.worldbank.org/JGAO5XE940, accessed 27 May 2012.

Worldbank.org. (n.d.a.). High-technology exports (% of manufactured exports), http://data.worldbank.org/indicator/TX.VAL.TECH.MF.ZS, accessed 27 May 2012.

Worldbank.org. (n.d.b.). KI and KEI indexes,
http://web.worldbank.org/WBSITE/EXTERNAL/WBI/WBIPROGRAMS/KFDLP/EX
TUNIKAM/0,,contentMDK:20584278~menuPK:1433216~pagePK:64168445~piPK:64
168309~theSitePK:1414721,00.html, accessed 27 May 2012

Worldbank.org. (n.d.b.). KI and KEI indexes,
http://web.worldbank.org/WBSITE/EXTERNAL/WBI/WBIPROGRAMS/KFDLP/EX
TUNIKAM/0,,contentMDK:20584278~menuPK:1433216~pagePK:64168445~piPK:64
168309~theSitePK:1414721,00.html, accessed 27 May 2012

Zikmund, A. G., & Babin, B. J. (2007). *Exploring Marketing Research, 9th ed.*, Mason, OH:
Thomson Southwestern.

Reflections from our Founding Editor

An Aneurysm from Preliminary Warnings to Recovery

Patrick Joynt

University of Reading, UK

On 8 March, 2010, I was with my wife, Unni, on a ski tour near our home in Nittedal, Norway. We had just started up the hill near the railroad crossing when we met a longtime friend of the family, Elisabeth Magnussen. Her first remark was to praise Unni for her "recovery" from a brain aneurysm four years earlier. "Look at you and how far you have come, it is a miracle!" And so we began writing the research case of Unni on Women's Day 2010. It is the story of a fantastic medical group in the USA, of a dedicated family, but most importantly, the story of a very determined woman who was on the verge of a tragedy that could have radically changed her life and that of her family.

Introduction

This text presents reflections concerning the case study of my wife's aneurysm from the preliminary warnings to recovery using different disciplinary angles. After interacting with my wife's doctors, the hospital administrative and research staffs, as well as with my family, I started to write notes about our journey. There were 250 pages of notes before my colleague and I decided to share them as a longitudinal 10-year case study in two international seminar presentations (IDRC, 2013; 2014), in addition to a journal article (Joynt, 2012). From this 10-year long case project, our largest contribution is made in the areas of the three T's (Things Take Time); Cognitive Development, cross-country skiing; Verbal Comprehension; Conceptual Reasoning; Boston Naming Task; Working Memory and Process Speed; Full IQ; and Behavioral

Reactions.

The main purposes and challenges of this reflective essay is the single case orientation and the use of a ten-year longitudinal framework for an academic audience. We are interested in "grounding" this work in the research process. There are several reasons for this. The story may help others to understand their situation and make improvements on the process involved. "Others" can include anyone involved in the process ranging from the hospital staff to the family and friends of the patient as well as other researchers. We also hope to make some key contributions to research from this work that has taken 10 years of written observations, feedback from circulated drafts and seminar presentations, key challenges involved, and the motivation to move and change some of the key boundaries of case and longitudinal studies as well as health research. With this in mind, a final section is added titled Key Contributions.

Literature Review

Using Case Studies in Research

Case studies are very popular at the university masters level (Yin, 2014, 5th edition), but more difficult to apply at the doctorate level (Morgan & Morgan, 2009; Reil & Leperi, 2011). At the doctorate level, Bevan (1997) and Homa (1999) studied the Leicester Hospital change case in the UK. It was the largest funded UK hospital change case study at that time. Felix (1999) did a doctorate case study on the BBC. The literature review also includes several recent case studies involving single samples at the individual analysis level. Joynt (2004) writing on MBRR (Management by Research Results) integrates the concept of action research with action learning using the framework developed by Eden and Huxham (1996). See Bowman-Peroit et al. (2013) for a meta-analytic review of single case research. Six doctor degree cases are reviewed here. The action research framework consists of 15 action research characteristics. Another valuable source for case studies is the Denzin and Lincoln Handbook of Qualitative Research (2005, 2015), One of the chapters in an earlier version (1994) by Stake is summarized here. Stake points out that case studies can be quantitative or qualitative or a combination of the two. He concentrated on the qualitative aspects of case studies in the Denzin and Lincoln 1994 Handbook. A qualitative case study can be described as having strong naturalistic, holistic, cultural, and phenomenological interests.

Stake (1994) identifies three types of case studies. The first is the intrinsic case study which is undertaken in order to obtain a better understanding of a particular case. The researcher temporarily subordinates other interests so that the case may reveal its story. The main purpose is not theory building, but a type of intrinsic interest. The second type of case study is the instrumental case study where a particular case is examined to provide insights into an issue or refinement of the theory involved. The third type of case study Stake calls a collective case study. In reality, this is an instrumental case study extended to several cases, and the cases may be similar or dissimilar, thus redundancy and variety each have a voice. The cases are often chosen so that one can obtain a better understanding and perhaps develop better theories.

Uniqueness in a case often involves: the nature of the case, the historical setting, the physical setting; other contexts such as economic, political, legal and aesthetic, and the informants through whom the case can be known. Often the researcher gathers data on all of the above. A case is often unique as it is a complex entity operating within a number of contexts. "Issues" are often used to describe the researcher's themes or dimensions. Often the researcher is asking "What issues bring out our initial concerns or dominant themes?"

Telling the Story is an important part of a case study! And the case often tells its own story! The researcher often becomes a teacher using two main pedagogical methods. Teaching didactically, the researcher is presenting what she or he has learned. In addition, in discovery learning the researcher provides material for students to learn on their own.

Some of the other items that Stake summarizes in his chapter are: triangulation; comparisons, methods of study, case selection; sampling within the case domain and ethics. Ethics deserve some attention here as the researcher has to make decisions on whose lives and expressions are portrayed, and the risk exposure and possible embarrassment to those involved. Limits of accessibility should be reviewed, and it is important for targeted persons to receive drafts of how they are perceived, quoted and presented; and the researcher should listen well to the feedback from targeted persons.

In closing his summary, Stake suggests the following stylistic options for case researchers:

- How much to make the report a story
- How much to compare with other cases
- How much to formalize generalizations
- How much to include description of the researcher(s) as a participant
- How much to anonymize….. or not

Sample (N = 1)

One of the earliest examples of using case research is Davidson and Costello (1969) where they made a very strong argument for a single case study (N = 1). Their work attempts to build bridges over the gap between experimental and clinical psychologists, and all the various sections have one thing in common: an interest in applying experimental methods to the study of the individual case. The authors begin with stating that "in spite of some enduring misconceptions, the application of statistical and experimental approaches to the single case is both possible and desirable. This application can require, however, a combination of flexible ingenuity and critical discipline that is not easy to achieve." (p. 1). What follows then, is the case of Peter involving a psychosomatic relationship, retardation, an individual case, and a case study in a behavioral analysis of psychotherapy. Many of the chapters in Davidson and Costello were first published in reputable journals.

The two key references used in both the background literature and in the methodology of this reflective essay were books written by Gawande (2002, 2007). Close to thirty cases are reviewed in the two books, and the various sections are labelled fallibility, mystery, uncertainty, diligence, doing right. The 2007 book concludes with a section called "Suggestions for becoming a Positive Deviant". Gawande "who manages to capture medicine in all of its complex and chaotic glory, and to put it, still squirming with life, down on the page… With this book Gawande inspires all of us, doctor or not, to be better" (Chen, 2011).

Moving on to some recent trends, a television show on Channel 4 in the UK entitled "Dispatches: Secret NHS (National Health Service) Diaries", was shown early in 2011. While the title was somewhat misleading, the programme filmed three people with terminal illnesses and their struggles with the health–care system. One story involved a case of hidden camera footage for nine days. The patient in question had a seizure on top of his pre-existing Parkinson's disease and kidney disease. The camera footage showed how impatient members of the caring professions can be when things do not run smoothly. The patient had difficulty swallowing his medicine. All the health staff had been informed of this, but some of the nurses took the patients problem as a personal affront. "We cannot help you if you don't help us"….. "Open your mouth!" as the frustration mounted…. "Open your mouth! Do you understand English!" The patient's daughter found that the patient could take his medicine if it was given to him in yogurt… but many of the staff persisted in trying to make the patient take the tablets dry.

In Norway, the newspaper Aftenposten ran an article on a Professor who had thirty-seven doctors from three different hospitals during a three-year illness. One could go on and on with single case examples. Chen (2011) argues that when patients share their stories, health management may improve. Homa (1999) found that one of the key contributions of his thesis was the need to appoint one main doctor and one main nurse for every patient. Hustvedt (2011) went one step further in her book by suggesting one be an expert with one's own sickness, as did Bolte Taylor (2008).

Finally, the intention in this reflective essay is to integrate some of the previous research methodology work done in the health sector. The strategy will be to present the situation under scrutiny using the notes and interviews taken, and then follow up with comments integrating some of this with previous health sector research as an instrumental case study (n = 1).

Recent research work in the case area involves Lenz (2015) who as guest editor of a journal issue devoted to case work, reviewed the case method, cognitive behaviour theory, strategies for research design, training practices, and counseling. Suffice it to say that the author has been a close observer during the entire case process which is now 10+ years and counting. In quantitative research, the main activities involve finding a group of valid and reliable variables and associated items (questions) that can be used to test some type of model possibly with independent and dependent variables in it. Statistics are then used to test if contributions can be made to the existing research in the area. A case study often involves more descriptive behaviour with fewer subjects in the sample. A better in depth analysis is usually the end result. With the case used in this essay, the intention is to include some of the quantitative work that has been done and make appropriate comments.

Health research

Evidence Based Research (EBR) has been a central theme in the health research areas in recent years, Ulrich, Zimring, Zhu, DuBose, Seo, Choi, Quau, Joseph (2008). This research strategy often requires time in the form of large samples (sample significance), and a statistical process of arriving at valid and reliable instruments that reflect the behaviour in question. In the research reported here, one can argue and show that there is an expansion of research alternatives using single samples as well as case studies. The time dimension has also been expanded to include 10 years and counting, rather than a single spot test or a study of two years or less. Little time will be spent on the intensive care part of the case in a hospital, rather we will concentrate on the behaviours tested in rehab as well as behaviours after leaving the two hospitals involved, in other words daily life at home.

While this part of the report will not dwell on an extensive literature review, one document stands out as a framework for the analyses that have been done in this case: "Cognitive Functioning and Health Related Quality of Life after Treatment of Intracranial Aneurysms", a thesis submitted by Haug and accepted by the Faculty of Medicine at the University of Oslo in 2009. More details will come later, but here are some of the main conclusions based on the key finding that cognitive functions improve at different rates:

1. Motor functions improve rapidly the first 6 months.
2. Memory functions first improve between 6 and 12 months.
3. Lower age is an important predictor for improvement in cognitive functions.
4. Many years (usually university level) of education is an important predictor for improvement in cognitive functions.
5. The importance of using more sensitive instruments in cognitive research.
6. All patients had a need for information and closer follow up of the emotional consequences.
7. Only 60% of patients return to work after 12 months post-operation. Most patients have a "good outcome" with only mild to moderate disabilities.
8. Psychologists should be an integrated part of the whole process.
9. Patients with aneurysms do not develop grave cognitive deficits.

In addition to the main thesis, four accepted refereed journal articles were also submitted by Haug (2009). While a thorough review of the literature will not be done here, the material will be integrated into the case as we move along. When appropriate, a more thorough literature review will be included in the other three sections that report on more detailed aspects of the case such as caretaking, hospital administration, and aneurysms (see Appendix 1). The reader is now entering the main aspects of the research case, and parts of this case involve people and organisations that performed above and below the standard norms. Because of this, the author/researcher must exercise caution on what is printed for public consumption.

Earlier, Haug's (2009) study "Cognitive Functioning and Health Related Quality of Life after Treatment of Intracranial Aneurysms" was reviewed. The following conclusions involving Haug (2009) are appropriate in the literature framework for this case:

1. The time course of cognitive recovery after aneurysmal SAH is heterogeneous with motor, psychomotor, visual and verbal, memory alterations, executive functions and intelligence as well as psychomotor functions convalescing within the first 6 months. Verbal memory often does not improve significantly until at least 6 months after the stroke. To conclude, the various cognitive functions have different time courses of recovery with verbal memory requiring the longest time. Unni's recovery tended to modify some of these results.

2. Surgical treatment of unruptured aneurysms (coiling) does not cause new cognitive deficits. The coiling technique was not applicable in this case as the "small" unruptured aneurysm Unni still has on the left side of her head has not been coiled, and tests over the first 9 years show no changes in size.

3. Often individuals who performed poorly after an SAH, were older. This appears to not be the case with Unni who was 67 years old in 2006.

4. Note that Haug reported that the cognitive problems were most likely caused by the bleed itself rather than the treatment of the ruptured aneurysm.

Other additional conclusions gathered from Haug's work with her colleagues were:

1. All patients have a need for information and a closer follow up of the emotional consequences. The main doctor is key here (Joynt, 2012)

2. Most patients have a "good outcome" with only mild to moderate disabilities.

3. Psychologists should be an integrated part of the whole program. This was done in the rehab stay for Unni.

4. Only 60% of patients return to work after 12 months post-operativity. Unni retired as a journal editor just weeks before her sickness. Within four years Unni was again active on two church boards and was involved in work using Latin, French, German, English, and Norwegian.

The cases in Gawande (2002) are real cases, but in order to tell them, many of the people involved had to be protected, thus names had to be changed. Medicine is a strange business as the stakes are high and many liberties are taken. People are drugged, manipulated, laid unconscious, and bodies are opened up. The gap between what medicine knows and what we aim for, complicates everything we do. Gawande tells stories in the capacity of a surgical resident, a laboratory scientist, a student of medicine, and philosopher. These are some of the perspectives the author brings with him in writing the complications associated with a typical case. Gawande focuses on three sections: the fallibility of the doctor, the mysteries and unknowns of medicine, and finally centers on uncertainty itself.

Gawande illustrates this with the example of a group of Harvard Business School researchers who had specialized in studying learning curves in industry. They followed eighteen cardiac surgeons and their teams as they took on the new technique of invasive cardiac surgery, and found striking differences in the speed with which the teams operated and learned. Contrasts between the quickest and slowest teams were startling. One of the most interesting chapters is titled "When Doctors Make Mistakes". Mistakes do happen, and they often go unseen. But not always, in one story a general surgeon left a large metal instrument in a patient's abdomen. In another, a cancer surgeon biopsied the wrong part of a woman's breast, and thereby delayed her diagnosis of cancer for months. In a story related to this research case, a man with abdominal pain in the emergency room was not given a CT scan, but was assumed to have a kidney stone. Eighteen hours later, a scan showed a rupturing abdominal aneurysm, and the patient died shortly afterwards. In a review of more than thirty thousand hospital admissions in New York State, nearly 4% of the hospital patients suffered complications from treatment. It was estimated that, nationwide, upward of forty-four thousand patients die each year as a result of errors in care.

Gawande (2002) supports the notion that medicine is a strange business, that learning curves are radically different in the same medical areas, and that some type of caretaker or outside observer is often an asset. Gawande (2007) followed up with another book called, "Better", some five years later. "In 2005, the United States spent more than two trillion dollars or one-sixth of all the money we have on health care." (p. 126) One of the key messages in the book is that "Better is Possible!". Gawande's five suggestions at the end of the book are worth repeating in the methodology and literature contexts for this case:

- Ask an unscripted question
- Don't complain
- Count something
- Write something (over 200 pages of notes have been used in the Unni case)
- Change

Bolte Taylor (2008) experienced a stroke while working at the Harvard Medical School where she was a brain scientist. Four hours after a major hemorrhage in the left hemisphere of her brain, Taylor could not walk, talk, read, write, or recall any of her life. The book is an integration of academic training and personal experiences and insights and the return to writing a book after the tragedy.

Chapter eight involves Bolte Taylor being moved to a Neurological Intensive Care Unit. The author sums up one of her key experiences as "I wish I had a dollar for every time I was given a neurological exam in that first 48 hours".(p 74) What was really happening is "my condition improved rapidly in some areas, but not at all in others". (p 75) It took Taylor eight years to completely heal her mind. Bolte Taylor titled the book "My Stroke of Insight". A good example of a long longitudinal case involving a sample of one (n = 1)

The following is a revised summary of the abstracts from three doctors I have supervised in the area of health administration: Bevan, Homa, and Playdon.

The Bevan (1997) UK thesis follows the temporal journey of a hospital's change programme over four years. Bevan was employed by the hospital as Reengineering Programme Leader, and she combines the change practitioner, researcher, and theory builder roles to create "actionable knowledge".

The change approaches offered by many re-engineering methodologists were insufficient to guide the hospital change process. In addition to situational process re-design, multifaceted changes were observed at leadership, internal community, and individual levels. Rather than the anticipated model of change intervention creating desired organisational behaviour, contradictory and shifting factors within the hospital both shaped and were shaped by the progress of the change programme. Paradox emerged as a major theme. The hospital exhibited both an ambition for radical change (creating tomorrow) and a need for significant stability (managing today).

The change programme did not result in the expected patient process configuration. Rather a hybrid specialty process model emerged. The adaptation of medical micro power was a significant factor. As a result, resources were re-organised around the patient's journey through the hospital. However, patient groups were segmented by the nature of medical input (specialty) rather than by common patient need or flow rate. Whilst contradictions within the hybrid create tensions towards a process form, the strength of specialty and functional perspectives in the wider healthcare system suggest that a further hybrid is more likely than a pure process configuration.

Homa's (1999) study of the UK National Health Service's (NHS) first complete hospital business process re-engineering programme provides a unique research insight. Further piquancy is added because the researcher is/was also the hospital's chief executive. This opened up a near ethnographic contextual examination of managing in the NHS at a time of tumultuous change. Operationalising the combined roles of chief executive and management researcher is one of this study's three contributions to management research. The research spans the period 1993 – 1996 when Homa was the head of the hospital studied.

Homa describes the hospital's early re-engineering programme results and consequential impact on the hospital's management structure and patient processes. The research methodology uses a combination of qualitative and quantitative approaches through the medium of four revelatory case studies taken from the Leicester Royal Infirmary's re-engineering programme. The case studies consider radical change attempted in four disparate areas of the hospital. Attention is given to factors that contribute to the assessed mobility of change evidenced in each case study. A predictive model is another of the study's major contributions. The variables that contribute to the constructs of health care process complexity and healthcare process implementation difficulty, are reviewed. The predictive model provides an approach in a highly contextual and sensitive manner. Through this analytical prism, emergent management theory is propounded. This is the study's third contribution to research.

The Playdon (2000) thesis used the ideas that the famous educationist A. S. Neill practiced at his Summerhill School, providing the model which was later used to develop an approach to democratic management at the Fairfield Centre, a primary healthcare centre in the socially disadvantaged area of Charlton, in South East London.

The thesis describes the process of developing, implementing, and running this process of democratic management. First, it considers the background for the work – the elusive nature of organisational democracy in today's management, which has made democracy a kind of "holy grail" of management, in contrast to the success of Summerhill's democracy for almost eighty years. Then it examines the nature of the narrative through which the story of Fairfield can be told, and in particular the role of the management consultant as researcher and author.

We will close this extended literature review with Doidge (2007). His conclusion was that the brain is more like an animated sea creature constantly changing and able to respond to injury with both functional reorganization as well as thinking into new anatomic configurations. Doidge calls his experimental data relatively primitive and calls for more research to be done in this area.

The Case

Aneurysms and Associated Behavioural Changes; Test Results

Unni was invited to take a battery of tests at the University of Wisconsin, Madison during 2011. The battery of tests took about 4 hours. Some of the key conclusions are presented below. But before we analyze the tests taken at the University of Wisconsin, Madison, one should look at some of the action research behaviours that Unni exhibited during the first five years after her three operations, that is behavours that have emerged over a period of the first 2 to 5 years. This study concentrates on the language behaviours that occurred after the initial stay (aphasia) in the hospital of a couple of months (see Karic, 2017) where memory deficit did not seem to be a problem, rather concentration and use of limited energy.

The Three T's (Things Take Time)

It has been a tradition to celebrate New Year's Eve at our cottage (hytte) in the mountains of Norway. Things are quiet and Unni and I enjoy the nature and spirit of winter in the Norwegian mountains. I also enjoy writing a letter to my four brothers and sisters in the US. It is usually 4 pages long, and I leave the last half page for Unni.

January 31st (2010) and three of my letters were finished. Unni wanted the radio music shut off so she could "concentrate" on her little note to our brothers and sisters. It took her about 10 to 20 minutes to write the short messages. Things Take Time (TTT), and Unni often concentrates on finding the right word, and the flow of the text in letter writing. Since we are on the subject of the radio, before her sickness (and recovery), Unni used to listen to the radio news rather than watch TV. She would combine listening to the radio with housework, etc.

A day later, Unni was busy writing letters to some of her Norwegian and German relatives that had not heard from her since 2006. They were 4 or 5 pages in length and in great detail both in German and Norwegian. Once she got started, things seemed to improve and progress rather rapidly. But she needed the uninterrupted time to write the letters. "Good style is essential".

Cognitive Development and Movies

Another of the cognitive changes that manifested itself after 2006, was Unni's reactions to movies. At first it seemed to be an energy/interest reaction – she did not have the energy, nor the interest to follow a movie from start to finish. However, what also seemed to emerge was a reaction against the violence that is/are part of a typical movie today. TV seemed a better alternative as she had to sit and put her legs up (doctor's orders) and use less energy with shorter programs.

But things change over time, and things progress as the notes from 2010 illustrate. It began with the French movie "Of God and Men" which was awarded the best French "movie of the year" in 2010. It is a story of eight catholic monks who have lived in their African monastery many years. The radical Muslim process in the countryside is a threat, and the first half of the movie deals with the monks deciding whether to stay on in Northern Africa or to move back to France. They decide to stay, and the movie ends with the kidnapping of six of them. The movie reports that they were killed by the rebels. It was a movie with many emotions, some strong, and Unni accepted the total experience.

A week later based on her initiative, we saw another movie "Another Year" by Mike Leigh. It was the story of an elderly UK couple who experienced everything from death to working in their garden which also involved taking a coffee break in their small "lean to" on the garden lot in the rain.

Finally, I turned on the TV movie channel two days later, and we started watching "Mission Impossible" with Tom Cruise. Action and violence were common, and Unni stayed with it for about an hour leaving to read in the kitchen with the comment "I'm wasting my time with this."

The above examples represent a gradual cognitive acceptance of the modern day movie with its action and violence. If one moves years back in time before her crisis, Unni did not like to watch the TV News with the typical menu of war, and natural catastrophes. Before her sickness, she usually listened to the radio news.

Much of the cognitive research on aneurysms has been quantitative and based on the first year after an aneurysm. The above movie cases suggest that some cognitions may develop over a period of years.

Cross Country Skiing

After we returned to Norway, some two and a half months after the initial three operations, the doctors recommended outdoor exercise. We were walking around our home in Nittedal once or twice a day. I had a bench about half way around the house, and Unni always needed a rest at the half way point. Snow came late in 2007, but when it came Unni mentioned her love of skiing "If they don't have cross country skiing in heaven, I ain't going". I called her doctor and asked if she could start skiing. He was very positive adding that it provided more motions and exercise than walking. I made a ski trail around the small pond near our home. The distance was about one third of a kilometer. Unni tried it out and was able to complete the entire round without a rest on her first try. Within three days, she was doing 3 rounds and asking about trying out one of the main trails nearby. Her first try on the main trail was perhaps too much as she became very tired when we returned home. In conclusion, cross country skiing was a major factor in her physical comeback.

In January, I was at the dentist one day. When I came home Unni had her ski outfit on and had been out cross country skiing. Below were her daily February results:

- 9 February: 8 kilometers
- 10 February: 8 kilometers
- 11 February: 10 kilometers
- 12 February: 13 kilometers
- 13 February Mother's Day in Norway: 10 kilometers with son Paul
- 14 February Valentine's Day: 10 kilometers
- 16 February: 7 kilometers

The following year, 2012, we had a warm winter in Norway so the skiing was not good especially in January, February and March. But the diary shows that Unni was averaging about 10 kilometers after a 5 kilometer start in the mountains in December. After that start, she reported she was not in shape and would have to train to achieve the level of the previous year. In the summer, we vacationed in the Madison, Wisconsin area, and Unni took a battery of psychological tests at the University Hospital as part of a research project. The test framework will be used with appropriate comments for the rest of this section.

Verbal Comprehension

The test was taken at the University of Wisconsin during one of our visits to the States. Unni scored in the top 18% of the Verbal Comprehension test. She was born in 1939 in Norway. Her mother was from Germany and her father Norwegian. She is fluent in the Scandinavian languages as well as German and English and does rather well in French. After the three operations in 2006, speaking in general was a problem, and speaking English was an added strain. I spoke Norwegian with her most of the time, and Doctor Baskaya recommended that the family fly over to support her. Daughters Kari and Maria came with their families, and the Norwegian Insurance company paid for their air tickets.

The report from the test she took during the summer of 2011 reported "The percentile scores are relative to neurologically healthy adults of Unni's age. Note that Unni's verbal and perceptual scores are quite high, despite many of the tasks were dependent on knowledge of American Culture and the English language. Her full IQ score is likely underestimated, because she took the test in her 3rd language." This report was done 4+ years after the aneurysm operations in 2006. Let us now take a look at her problems with language in the rehab time a month after the operations.

Unni's biggest problem in the rehab was with the "language help" she was given. Often the language hour came after her hour of exercise walking, and she did not have sufficient energy to respond to all the language exercises. So she often made the choice of a very limited answer or not answering at all. Some of the discussion topics were rather naive, and afterwards she would tell me " I didn't want to waste my time and energy with them." I tried to explain that Unni and I had good conversations on ……. topics where she used both Norwegian and English. Often I felt the hospital language assistant was not interested in this information, and she would reply that her tasks were "based on research. " This tended to frustrate both Unni and myself. I reported this to the head of the department that more understanding and improvements in the tasks used would have helped Unni a great deal.

Normally Unni is the more extroverted of the two of us and enjoys a good conversation. As time passed from the events at the end of 2006, we found that:

1. Verbal Comprehension returned to almost normal for Unni within a year or two for English and Norwegian. She did not get that much practice in German, but the long German letter to her relatives in 2010 is evidence that this language was also being used.
2. Writing abilities were not used that much during the first year, but they have returned in the second year, and the long Christmas letters reported above is evidence of this. She still uses the "draft" stage in some of her writing, but it is not as common as it was the first couple of years.
3. Movies were not on my research agenda during the first years after the three operations, but the movie interest returned after about three years. We see an average of a movie a month on the town, and enjoy a good one now and then on TV.
4. Language assistance – if the truth is to be told – Unni has been a major asset in my achieving professor status at several Universities in Europe and the USA. I didn't start school in Iowa until I was close to 8 years as we lived too far from the school. As a result of this late start,

many of my fellow students had already learned to read and write, my parents were often called in at the end of the year to "review my marginal status." In addition to a slow start, I have dyslexia tendencies which run in my family. Unni has been my "editor" for many years and has returned to this status in the past couple of years. She is an outstanding mentor.

5. Community Integration. In 2013 Unni was asked to write a paper on Dorthy Day who is being considered for sainthood in the Catholic Church. She also made a 2-hour presentation of the paper to a seminar where there were 50+ participants from the church organization where Unni was elected a board member. She has also been very active with a church women's group and a group from her High School days. She is also very active with the Joynt family in Norway which now numbers over 20.

Perceptual Reasoning

Unni scored in the top 25% in this test which is not surprising. She did not read newspapers and news journals for about a year or two after the operations. Once she began reading, her time and energy used on these activities increased. She now reads about 3 newspapers on an average for each day. Her favorite programs are the news on radio and TV as well as the news hours. In many respects, these programs are exercises in perceptual reasoning.

Boston Naming Task

Unni did well in this test scoring in the top 50%. My main professor job and our main abode has been in England for the last 15 years, and it is interesting to see how she reacted to an American test in her third language, maybe fourth, if you accept the notion that England and America are two countries separated by a common language. The three T's mentioned earlier in this section had a new dimension when Unni took this test. Unni tended to speed up on her answers. Her behaviour reminded me of the 2006 rehab language sessions where she had to choose between answering and using energy, or not answering and saving energy. Some of the items in the test were given interesting "suggested responses" (like bed… is it a piece of furniture or something to sleep on; is a house a building; is a volcano a kind of mountain – some are not on the top of mountains; palette – do only artists use it – our grandchildren are great painters?) was some of the feedback I received from Unni after she had taken the test.

Unni worked as editor of St. Olavs magazine for over 20 years, and one of her key competencies was knowledge of languages and the details involved in translation and summarizing. Daughter Kari is senior editor for one of the most successful publishing houses in Norway. Much of her language talents come from her mother.

Working Memory and Process Speed

When it comes to speed, we have mentioned the reaction "I have to think about it" earlier. Unni tended to score in the top 60+% for both of these tests. I do know that her memory of remembering things that happened a year or a month ago has returned. Much of this happened in the first year. Her working memories often have to do with social activities. Last night she caught the main news on TV in a translation mistake concerning a behavior attributed to Norwegian customs on Women's Day. At the end of the program the newscaster also corrected the mistake. Unni is very good at details!

When asked to repeat and then put lists of numbers backwards, one should realize that this was an exercise done in her third language which could tend to slow down the results. Unni was rather frustrated with this exercise.

Full IQ

Unni achieved one of the highest averages in her classes at the University of Oslo as well as in High School. I am not sure the test reflects her ranking in the top 45%. Perhaps there are other biases here. Speaking of biases, we found a number of interesting questions in the test. When Unni was asked to identify Martin Luther King she went silent and had to think. After some time, she replied that he was the father to Martin Luther King jr. Junior was forgotten when the question was asked. Other NAMES used in the IQ test were Hamlet, Shakespeare, Lincoln and Gandhi. Are these the right questions to ask a Norwegian on an IQ test. We noted that about half the patients during her stay at the University of Wisconsin Hospital Rehab were from other countries.

On a TV program a week ago, the BBC was doing a program on the Amish in the USA. The reporter asked a group of about 5 Amish men if they knew who James Bond was? To help he added, 007. No one knew.

As a final test note, Unni refused to do the $2000 game with four decks of cards. She is and has never been a gambler. Refusing even to take a gambling test! "I had had enough of the whole testing business".

Other Research Conclusions

Haug (2009) in her doctorate thesis, with 3 associated published articles, studied the cognitive functions and quality of life after treatment of intracranial aneurysms. Her sample involved observations of patients at 3, 6 and 12 months' post aneurysm. In her review, she found that the overall mortality rate was close to 50% with 46% dying within the first 30 days after the initial aneurysm. Other information from her review of the research, showed that cognitive dysfunction was the most common form of impairment. She also found that deficits which lasted more than one or two months following surgery, were likely to remain. However, few studies have evaluated cognitive functioning in the same individual at more than two points in time. IQ tests of patients were close to the population mean, however, memory was significantly poorer. This may be due to damage of the frontal lobe, which can also cause executive and personality behaviour problems

Interestingly, Haug (2009), who defended her thesis in Norway, also reported that the tests used in research were often dated, difficult to change, and did not take into account advances in operation procedures. She also reported that many of the studies had been done years ago, and that older tests of executive functions and memory do not seem to be able to capture subtle differences in function among good outcome patients. These limitations were also found in the Unni case. And we had difficulty being heard when we brought up these criticisms to the staff involved.

In one of the four published papers included in the thesis, Haug reported that half of 70 survived the bleed and 26 were tested. Half of these had good physical and cognitive outcomes. In the Unni case, it is our view that she has had good physical and cognitive outcomes. Perhaps more case studies over a period of say 5 years may help us to understand the period after the operation for an aneurysm better.

Doidge (2007) applied many of the action research criteria mentioned earlier. Doidge is a Canadian psychiatrist and an award winning science writer. Using the concept of "neuroplasticians" he presents several cases. A woman who feels she is in constant free fall, puts a set of electrodes on the surface of her tongue and a wired hard hat on her head. Soon the feeling of free fall stops. The computer system is sending the correct signals to her brain via her tongue. After a year of this exercise, she no longer needs the computer.

In another case a surgeon in middle age suffers a stroke and can no longer use one arm. In a rehab clinic he is given the task of cleaning tables. At first the task is impossible with both arms, then slowly the bad arm remembers the skill. From these preliminary experimental cases other research may show us how to reconstruct creativity, love, anger, and grief. The brain is organic and malleable as Unni's case also tends to show.

We leave the reader with this thought as we close this section. All patients begin as storytellers (Gawande, 2002, 2007; Doidge, 2007; Boltr Taylor, 2008; Chen, 2011). Long before they see a doctor they become narrators of the pains and hurts they are experiencing. Why not use them more in the research which is what action research is all about (Stake, 1994; Eden and Huxham, 1996; Joynt, 2004).

Conclusions After Four Years, Unni's Reactions

I had an interview one afternoon in August 2010 with Unni in a park near our apartment in Oslo. I asked her for the positive and negative experiences she has had since the crisis of 2006. Many of them are supported with the case presented in this reflective essay. Here is a short summary of what Unni told me:

On the Plus Side:

1. Most of my language abilities and talents are still there.
2. I can take a long walk, I can walk for hours
3. I have the ability to think
4. How fortunate I am
5. I try to focus on what I can do rather than on what I cannot do
6. The family rallied and supported me, and this assisted me in my challenge.

7. A deepened relationship with Pat

8. Skiing up to 20km per day

9. I make a good dinner although I often have to think and plan more than in the past

On the Negative Side:

1. Resigned to the fact that you are not as strong and agile as you used to be

2. The operations tended to compound my sleeping problems

3. I wanted to be a full time grandmother… instead I only have energy to be a half time grandmother.

4. My singing voice has gone down one octave, but this is minor, and aging may be a factor here.

Conclusions After Ten Years, Unni's Reactions

After reviewing a draft of this reflective essay, Unni and I have discussed her ten year reactions during the last few days. Here is her written summary which integrates the "plus" and "negative" views:

It is difficult to differentiate between what might be a "getting old factor" and factors associated with the "aftermath of my operations and recovery from 2006".

1. I still have sleeping problems at night, and they are rather worse than better.

2. More anxiety with worries – death is drawing nearer, sickness and death among close friends and relatives.

3. Enjoy being able to contribute to our eleven grandchildren from age 24 to 2.5 years. We are with our youngest grandchild, little Isak, most days.

4. Thanks to you dear Pat – for your patience, encouragement, support, and understanding.

Key Contributions

We conclude this section of the research by integrating the five most important conclusions and contributions with the appropriate prior research results. Hopefully this will provide a deeper in depth understanding of the dynamics involved in this reflective essay of the ten-year case study.

1) One thing at a time supplemented with the 3 Ts (Things take time). Haug (2009) used time dimensions of 6 and 12 months as well as 2 years. Some of the observations of Unni were integrated with the literature review. Here the interest involves Unni moving away from taking a long time to make decisions or not making a decision to being more dynamic as time moved on. From the interviews with Unni, we found that she often used priorities thus using her available energy in a realistic way (Gawande, 2002, 2007)

She achieved "normal time behaviour" in some areas after about 4 or 5 years. It often occurred with an unexpected challenge such as the cross-country ski incidents which was discussed earlier. In year 8, she made a one-and-a-half-hour presentation on Dorthy Day for close to 50 people in an all-day religious seminar. Most people would conclude that Unni is normal today. But at times, she does take time especially when she is tired which was another result after her 3 major operations many years ago. Taylor (2008) was another example of where major time changes started taking place after 5 years. This study also involved N = 1.

In summary, the guidelines provided by Stake (1994) and Bolte Taylor (2008) provided the methodology guidelines for the Unni case involving close to 10 years of collecting observations which provide interesting conclusions in the areas of Things Taking Time.

2) Cognitive Development involves research in the area of cognitive psychology focusing on all human activities relating to knowledge. Often this is done by experiments and tests designed to measure and analyze human behaviour in carrying out a wide range of mental tasks (Gawande 2002, 2007, Haug 2009, Bolte Taylor 2008). Perceptual reasoning, Boston naming task, and Full IQ were given to Unni in 2011 as part of a University of Wisconsin Hospital research effort. Unni scored above average for normal persons in every area some 5 years after her 3 operations. Additional cognitive development information was given such as cross-country skiing motivation and abilities, particular attention to details, language abilities in German, Norwegian and English.

She also had appointments, which included a review of her progress, with her American and Norwegian doctors. NORMAL BEHAVIOUR seems to be the major conclusions and contribution here.

3) Verbal Comprehension is a key conclusion and contribution in this research. Unni has a German mother and a Norwegian father. She also has an advanced degree from the University of Oslo in Literature. After the 3 operations at the University Hospital in Madison, Wisconsin, she had trouble speaking at all at first, and usually spoke to me in Norwegian and had limited English conversations with hospital staff. After two years we were back into the habit of using both Norwegian and English in our daily conversations. In terms of writing it took about 3 years before she started writing long letters again. It was also in this third year that she resummed writing to her German relatives. In year 7 she started writing a 12-page manuscript on Dorthy Day, the well know American, who is being mentioned as a Saint candidate in the Catholic Church. She presented the paper in 2012 to an audience of over 50 using two hours.

In conclusion, age behaviour versus aneurysm caused behaviour is a real challenge, especially when the person is over 70 years of age. With this in mind, we concentrated initially on the first two to three years as Haug (2009) and many others have done. However, Bolte Taylor (2008) found most of her development occurring four or more years after the heart attack that paralyzed her. Unni experienced somewhat the same late recoveries.

4) Perceptual Reasoning is the test where Unni scored in the top 25%. In many respects, the qualitative methodological aspects of this study help us to understand this concept better. Today some ten years later, Unni has to deal with 3 children and their spouses as well as 11 grandchildren living in the Oslo area. She is also very active in two women groups and a member of the board in a church organization. She reads 3 newspapers and always has a book in hand. Earlier it was mentioned that she had some difficulties communicating as it took so much energy. That is no longer the case as she is a very updated modern female. She is well aware of her aches and pains and enjoys a concert once a month in Oslo. She is eye, nose, ear, and feeling minded. She is with it! And has pasted 75 years of age a few years ago. She also has to deal with a sister who has Alzheimer's, the family farm in Southern Norway, her wedding present – a cottage in Wisconsin with seven bedrooms that the five core members of the family now own jointly, a hytte (cottage) in the Norwegian mountains

In the literature review section Haug (2009), Gawande (2002, 2007), Bolte Taylor (2008), and the tests Unni took at the University of Wisconsin in 2011 along with 10 years of research oriented observations using single case study methodology, has helped us to understand the meanings of perceptual reasoning.

5. N = 1. The single organization studies were mainly hospital studies as well as the BBC, Bevan (1997), Homa (1999), Felix (1999). Individuals organization studies included Davidson and Costello (1969), Gwande, (2002,2007), Chen (2011), Bolte Taylor (2008) and Linz (2015). Most case recommendations suggesting less than a year or two years maximum, Yin (2014), Stake (1994). Many of the above contributions involved more than a couple of years which is the best argument for adopting a longer time frame in some research.

References

Action Medical Research site on Wikipedia, 2015.

Aftenposten Newspaper, (20ll), articles: Sykehus er lik en produksjonsbedrift, Alle har krav på en fastlege, Skal slippe mange leger.

Bevan, H. (1997), Managing Today While Creating Tomorrow: Actionable Knowledge for Organisational Change in an NHS Hospital, Doctor Thesis from Brunel University, UK.

Bolte Taylor, J. (2008), My Stroke of Insight; a Brain Scientist's Personal Journey, Hodder Publishing, London.

Bowman-Peroit, L. , Davis, H., Vannest, K., Wiliams, L., Greenwood, C., and Parker, R. (2013) Academic benefits of peer tutoring ; A meta-analytic review of single –case research. School Psychology Review,42, 39-53.

Channel 4, UK, (2011), Dispatches: Secret National Health Service Diaries.

Chen, Pauline, (Feb. 10, 2011), When Patients Share their Stories Health May Improve, New York Times.

Davidson, P.O. and Costello, C.G. (1969), N=1: Experimental Studies of Single Cases, Van Nostrand Reinhold Company, London.

Denzin, N.K. and Lincoln, Y.S. editors, (latest edition), Handbook of Qualitative Research,

London, Sage Publishing; (Stake 1994) (2nd edition 2015)

Doidge, N. (2007), The Brain that Changes Itself; Stories of Personal Triumph from the Frontiers of Brain Sceince, Viking Press.

Eden, C. and Huxham,c. (1996) Action Research for the Study of Organisations, in S. Clegg, C. Hardy and W.Nord (eds) Handbook of Organisation Studies, Sage, Beverly Hills, CA.

Felix E. (1999) BBC Case Study, Doctor Thesis from Brunel Universkity, UK.

Gawande, A. (2002), Complications, A Surgeon's Notes on an Imperfect Science, Henry Holt and Company, New York.

Gawande, A. (2007), Better, A Surgeon's Notes on Performance, Picardo, New York.

Haug, T. K. (2009), Cognitive Functioning and Health Related Quality of Life after Treatment of Intracranial Aneurysms, University of Oslo Ph.D. Thesis.

Homa, P. (1999), Re-engineering The Leicester Royal infirmary Healthcare Process, Doctor Thesis from Brunel University, UK.

Hustvedt, S. (2011), Den Skjelvende Kvinnen, Aschehoug, Oslo.

Joynt, P. et al. (editors Coghlan, Dromgoole, Joynt and Sorensen) , (2004), Managers Learning in Action, Thomson Publishing, London.

Joynt, P. I wish to thank the 50 doctor associates, now Doctors and Professors, who studied with me as their supervisor, for all the insights and learning they have given me.

Joynt, P. (2012), The Main Doctor – Alongitudinal Case Study: An Aneurysm from Preliminary Warnings to Recovery, Volume 1, Number 1.

Karic, T. (2017) Early rehabilitation after aneurysmal subarachnoid hemorrhage. University of Oslo Ph.D. Thesis

Lenz, S. (Guest Editor, 2015). Using Single-Case Research Designs to Demonstrate Evidence for Counseling Practices, Journal of Counseling and Development, October Volume 93

Morgan, Dl L., and Morgan, R. K. (2009) Single-case research methods for the behavioral and health sciences. Thousand Oaks, CA; Sage

Playdon, Zoe Jane, (2000), The Fairfield Centre: A Case Study in Democratic Management, Doctor Thesis from Brunel University, UK.

Riel, M. & Leperi, K. (2011) A Meta-Analysis of the outcomes of Action Research, Paper presented at the American Educational Research Association Conference, April, 2011, New Orleans.

Stake (1994) See Denzin and Lincoln (1994)

Ulrich, R., Zimring, C., Zhu, X., DuBose, J., Seo, H., Choi, Y, Quan, X., Joseph,A., (2008) A Review of the Research Literature on Evidence-Based Healthcare Design- April, Vol 1, no 3.

Yin; Robert K. (2014), Case Study and Applied Research, 5th edition, Sage Publications, London.

APPENDIX 1

The full report of the five papers involved in this case study

1. INTRODUCTION 2012, 51 pages

The entire introduction document could be considered as a small book as each section can stand on its own. The overall intention was to produce several research oriented papers as well as complete documentation for the family and caretakers involved in the case. The key sections included: Family support and interaction, suggested refinements to previous research on aneurysms, the single case methodology, the hospital administration processes in Norway and the USA, the role of the caretaker/giver, aneurysms and associated behavioural changes, the role of the main doctor involved

2. THE MAIN DOCTOR – A LONGITUDINAL CASE STUDY; AN ANEURYSM FROM PRELIMINAR WARNINGS TO RECOVERY

Published (2012) in the Journal of international Doctorial Research (JIDR) pages 52 – 73.
Practical and Theoretical Conclusions:
The main doctor made key decisions in the three operations performed; the rehabilitation process; flight back to Norway; and follow – ups. Family support as Doctor Baskayas letter to the insurance company involved resulted in the company paying for the flights from Norway to the US Hospital for our two daughters. Finally, the key culture in the University Hospital "How can we do things better".

3. ANEURYSIMS AND ASSOCIATED BEHAVIOURAL CHANGES

This reflective essay

4. FAMILY SUPPORT AND INTERACTION, 28 pages

This section is a documentation of Unni's 50 day stay at the USA hospital as well as the trip back to the hospital in Norway. It is intended as a record of the key events in 2006 when Unni had her aneurysm. The aspect of caretaking/ caregiving has been updated in 2017.

5. SUMMARY BOOKLET

To be completed later.